Second Manifesto for Philosophy

Second Manifesto for Philosophy

ALAIN BADIOU

Translated by Louise Burchill

polity

First published as *Second manifeste pour la philosophie* © Librairie Arthème Fayard, 2009

This English edition © Polity Press, 2011

Liberté • Égalité • Fraternité
RÉPUBLIQUE FRANÇAISE

This book is supported by the French Ministry of Foreign Affairs, as part of the Burgess programme run by the Cultural Department of the French Embassy in London (www. frenchbooknews.com)

Ouvrage publié avec le concours du Ministère français de la Culture - Centre national du livre

Published with the assistance of the French Ministry of Culture - National Centre for the Book

Polity Press
65 Bridge Street
Cambridge CB2 1UR, UK

Polity Press
350 Main Street
Malden, MA 02148, USA

ISBN-13: 978-0-7456-4861-3
ISBN-13: 978-0-7456-4862-0(pb)

A catalogue record for this book is available from the British Library.

Typeset in 12 on 15 pt Garamond Light
by Servis Filmsetting Ltd, Stockport, Cheshire
Printed and bound in Great Britain by MPG Books Group Limited, Bodmin, Cornwall

For further information on Polity, visit our website: www.politybooks.com

Contents

Acknowledgements

Schemas

The two paintings found on the inside covers of this book (for one can without exaggeration speak of paintings) were executed, on the basis of my own clumsy pen sketches, by the artist Monique Stobienia. *Schema 2* had been handed out in my seminar, which Monique Stobienia attended. Interested in incorporating philosophical concepts within contemporary work on visibility, she then elaborated an astonishing series of variations of this schema (in truth, seven different series), which ranged from a version as close as possible to – although already far beyond – the original (this being the painting reproduced here for *Schema 2*) to constructions where the lines' structured force merges with an original conception of colour and a sort of underlying fantastical landscape. I have, moreover, reserved one

vi

of these variations for the cover of this book, for this intermixing furnishes me with a sensible idea of what philosophy, in the grip of its own appearing, inflicts upon the concepts that it, in addition, exhibits. In the light of all this, I commissioned Monique Stobienia to freely execute *Schema 1*.

I would like here to warmly and philosophically thank this artist. I, moreover, believe that this collaboration, so generously initiated by her musing upon and experimenting with my work – as she had already done for that of Jacques Derrida – will continue under different forms.

Translator's Preface: A Manifest Power of Elevation

Like a number of other philosophers of his generation – notably, Deleuze and Derrida – Badiou has emphatically asserted the primacy of syntax over semantics and etymology. Just as Deleuze discerned the 'dynamic lines' of syntax to veritably chart the movement of the concept[1] and Derrida was to refer even the 'indecidability' of words with multiple meanings less to 'semantic infinity' than to the 'formal and syntactic practice composing and decomposing' them,[2] so too, for Badiou, that which is determining in the transmission of thought is the network of relations in, and by, which concepts are arrayed and articulated, and not any form of speculative exposition of an originary or substantial semantic core. Badiou's finding himself in the company of Deleuze and Derrida in this respect accords, moreover, with the article he wrote on the French language for a 'European Vocabulary of Philosophies', which argues French philosophy as a whole to be entirely guided by the conviction that 'only by complying to syntactic constraints can one give free rein to the Idea'.[3] There is, then, no privilege granted to the national dialect, no thinking contemplation of words' origin, their semantic equivocity or speculative substance. 'France has always scoffed at [. . .] "the proof by etymology"',[4] just as Badiou himself ridicules all those – German for the most part – who would claim for their language a philosophical depth uniquely consonant with the saying of being. That there is no substantial affinity between thought and a national dialect or, in other words, that concepts are themselves 'indifferent to language', does not, however, exclude diverse languages from differentially orienting the movement or tonality of the concepts they convey – after all, French philosophy's privileging of syntax over substance is, for Badiou determined by the French language's particularity of having 'syntax as its essence'. Certainly, an 'amplitude of syntax'[5] finely orchestrates Badiou's own argumentation, as many a translator has remarked in their prefaces to his works in English. In translating Badiou, one's predominant concern is, indeed, to respect the relations established between elements of a concept or between one concept and another, be this by scrupulously adhering (as far as possible) to the original structure of his sentences or by recomposing the latter, with a view to maintaining the formal consecution of elements, if not their sequential order, within a different syntactical system – English being, in fact, a more '*syn*tactic' or explicitly 'coordinated' language than French, which privileges *para*tactic constructions, such as juxtaposition ellipsis, and the omission of conjunctions. Be this as it may, however, the preeminent problem posed by the translation of Badiou's *Second Manifesto for Philosophy* was well and truly one of terminology, necessitating attention, notwithstanding Badiou's disapprobation, not only to semantic and etymological networks but, beyond this, to exemplary claims of 'proof by speculative substance'. That the terms involved – primarily, the French verb *relever* and its nominal form *relève* – represent one of the most important notions in Badiou's metaphysics, and perhaps even 'the whole of philosophy', will become clear in what follows. Before attending, though, to the inflexion Badiou gives to the technical use of *relever/relève*, we need to rapidly chart these terms' 'conceptual history' in order to situate the choices leading us to render them, contrary to convention, by two 'everyday' English locutions: 'to raise up' and 'raising up'.

Relever and *relève* first entered the philosophical lexicon in 1967, when Jacques Derrida proposed them as translations of two terms that have undoubtedly given rise to the most sustained and documented of all debates around philosophical translation, namely Hegel's *aufheben* and *Aufhebung*. Literally meaning 'to lift up', *aufheben* also contains the 'double meaning' of 'to preserve' and 'to put an end to', as illustrated by such (supposedly) idiomatic German expressions as *Konfitüren für den Winter aufheben*, where the fruit that has been accordingly *aufgehoben* by its transformation into potted jam may be understood as modified by a 'form of negation', assuring its preservation under conditions different from those characterizing it at the start. That one and the same word of a natural language should conjoin two opposite and *concurrent* meanings was, in Hegel's view, a chance for philosophical thought in so far as such words would, 'in themselves', have 'a speculative meaning'. In the case of *aufheben,* according to the Remark in the *Science of Logic* devoted to the expression, such a meaning would consist of nothing other than 'a fundamental determination which repeatedly occurs throughout the whole of philosophy' – though what exactly such a determination entails is notoriously left unspecified by Hegel,[6] who limits himself to stressing, in this respect, *aufheben*'s impossibility, qua 'mediation', to be conflated with the concept of *nothing*: 'what is *aufgehobene* is at the same time preserved; it has only lost its immediacy but it is not on that account annihilated'.[7] That said, despite the absence of any precise definition in Hegel's terminological remark, there is no doubting the fundamental role attributed to the operation of *Aufhebung* within the Hegelian dialectic: it is the very process by which contradiction between opposites is resolved by negating the concepts in question and transmuting them such that they are raised up and conserved within a 'greater whole', revealing the identity in all difference.

The difficulty posed by the translation of *aufheben* and *Aufhebung* consists, of course, in finding a word in another language with the dual signification of 'to put an end to', or 'suppress', and 'to preserve'. With such an enterprise often being deemed impossible – and by no one more systematically than Derrida himself, who habitually qualifies his propositions of *relever* and *relève* as 'quasi-translations' or 'translations-interpretations'[8] – many of Hegel's translators have turned away from 'ordinary language' to either renounce translating the terms altogether or to avail themselves of technical neologisms or obsolete terms of Latin filiation (at least in the case of English and French) whose etymology purportedly encompasses the conjoined contra-dictory meanings of Hegel's German. 'To sublate' and 'sublation', which were first proposed as translations for *aufheben* and *Aufhebung* by J. H. Stirling in the mid-1800s and have since become the conventional – if by no means consensual – English-language rendering, are examples of the etymological exhumation of a little used extant term, even if Stirling simply imposed, in fact, the extra semantic dimension of 'to preserve' upon the verb 'sublate', used with the sense of 'to deny' in nineteenth-century logic texts.[9] The French *sur-primer* (proposed by Jean Wahl in 1966) and *sursumer* and *sursomption* (Yvon Gauthier in 1965) illustrate, on the other hand, the recourse to neologisms, which also pre-eminently relies, of course, on etymological considerations even if drawing at times upon conceptual inter-refer-entiality. Whatever the underpinnings of such propositions, however, their evident shortcoming is to represent *aufheben* and *Aufhebung* – two perfectly ordinary German terms – as far more esoteric than they are and, correlatively, through their own lack of idiomatic resonance, to func-tion as mere 'place-holders', referring by conven-tion to the German words they stand in for. By completely eliding the speculative operation by which Hegel's text seizes upon the philosophi-cal resources of an everyday word, the recourse to technical neologisms or obscure Latin deriva-tions seems, when all is said and done, to lend credence to the contentious proclamation (by both Hegel and Heidegger) of German's 'intrinsic' philosophical propensity, such that *aufheben*'s 'intranslatability' into other natural languages would ultimately reveal itself to be a 'failure' not merely of translation but of these languages' amenability to thought as such.

Given that the (speculative) stakes of *aufheben*/*Aufhebung*'s translation equally bear, therefore, on the principle of 'universalism' that Badiou, in his article mentioned above on the French language, opposes to any and all claims of a linguistic condition being attached to thought's formation, transmission or reception – such as would signal 'a privileged relation between Being and a national language'[10] – it is not surprising to find Badiou himself take up a position in this debate on philosophical translation. While quoting the *Science of Logic* in the translation by P.-J. Labarrière and G. Jarcyzk throughout his chapter on Hegel in *Being and Event*, Badiou specifies in a note his objection to the translators' rendering of *aufheben* by *sursumer* – a neologism which, formed by contrast with Kant's *subsumieren* ('to subsume' in English; 'subsumer' in French), would purportedly convey the 'most direct sense of the *Aufhebung*', namely, the 'positivity of the negativity in the very movement of its accomplishment', through its etymologically informed reference to 'a part's being taken up within the process of totalization'.[11] Whether or not *sursumer* succeeds in capturing the sense of *aufheben* carries, however, little weight in the verdict Badiou delivers as to its adequation as a translation: 'the substitution of a technical neologism in one language for an everyday word from another language appears to me to be a renunciation rather than a victory'.[12] With the task of the translator thus firmly transposed to the terrain of 'everyday language',[13] Badiou then sets down the terms he considers to have triumphed in the battle for the transmission of thought: 'I have thus taken up J. Derrida's suggestion: *relever, relève.*'[14]

Now, as an 'everyday' French word, the verb *relever* has a vast number of meanings, of which we need indicate here solely the main semantic clusters:[15] 'to lift up' (to right, to help [back] up, to raise, to bring to the surface, etc.); 'to pull up' (to turn up, to roll up, etc.); 'to put higher' (to raise, to heighten . . .); 'to restore' (to rebuild, to put back on its feet . . .); 'to increase' (to put up, to boost . . .); 'to enhance' (to put into relief, to season . . .); to relieve (to take over from . . .); 'to remark' (to point out, to take up . . .); 'to take down' (to note [down], to record . . .); 'to react to'; 'to collect' (to take in, to pick up . . .); 'to release' (to relieve . . .); 'to recover from'; and 'to come under'. The noun *relève* – a late derivation from the verb – has, on the contrary, a considerably more curtailed semantic range, being restricted to the senses of 'taking over from', 'replacing', or 'relieving' someone or something in a function or task, on the one hand, and of 'the time that such a replacement lasts', on the other. Referring thereby to a process of substitution which is no less one of preservation, as seen exemplarily in expressions such as *la relève de la garde* ('the changing of the guard') or *la relève d'un soldat* ('relieving a soldier [on duty]'), the sense of replacement paramount in *relever*'s nominal form is obviously determining for Derrida's proposing the verb as a translation for Hegel's *aufheben*. Encompassing in itself, as it were, the contradictory meanings of 'to suppress', and 'to preserve', this value of substitution comes to complement that of 'to lift' (*lever* corresponding in this respect to the German *heben*), such that the French word would effectively seem to combine what Derrida, when first proposing the Hegelian translation in his 1967 article 'The Pit and the Pyramid', was to describe as 'the senses in which one can be both raised in one's functions and relieved of them, replaced in a kind of promotion, by that which follows and relays or relieves one'.[16] In short, to cite Derrida again, though this time from a text on translation written some thirty years later, *relever*, no less than *aufheben,* would thus conjoin in 'a single word, the double motif of the elevation and the replacement that preserves that which it denies or suppresses, preserving what it causes to disappear'.[17]

The elegance of Derrida's translation, with its maintenance of the verb meaning 'to lift', its prefix 're' gesturing towards the 'up' of the German 'auf' through its function as an intensifier, and the conjoined meanings of suppression/conservation conveyed in its sense of 'replacement', should not, however, cause us to overlook what it entails by way of a certain 'forcing', or over-determination, of the French term. Despite Derrida's emphasizing 'the double theme of elevation and replacement', the sense of 'raising up' is, in fact, as absent from the verb *relever* in contexts pertaining to 'someone being relieved from their post' (where one understands the person to be simply divested of their responsibilities without any 'kind of promotion') as it is from its nominal form in expressions such as *relève de la garde*. The 'combined senses' – 'to lift up', 'to replace' – that Derrida attributes to *relever* are, in *everyday* language, strictly speaking, separate ones accruing to different occurrences of the verb; only in the technical use Derrida himself makes of the term are they effectively 'conjoined' as simultaneous values.

That said, it is less Derrida's 'speculative seizure' of an 'everyday word' in itself that is of pertinence here than the singular emphasis he places, as confirmed by both his 1967 gloss and the 1998 article dealing with translation, on the 'theme' of elevation. Certainly, this is a theme that, beyond its evident presence in *aufheben*'s ordinary sense, is undeniably encompassed by the *process* of the *Aufhebung* operative within (Hegel's) thought: as a movement in which a concept's immediate determination via its opposition to something other is negated by being taken up within a superior determination of self-identity, the *Aufhebung* does, indeed, result in a synthesis that is *higher than*, or *the truth of*, that which was given at the start. Yet such a 'raising up' is in no way thematically singled out by Hegel, who, in his terminological remarks on *aufheben*, doesn't even mention, in fact, its sense of 'to lift up'. The latter would, as such, seem almost a mere vehicle for the speculative chance having endowed, in Hegel's view, this 'one and the same word' with the twofold sense 'suppression' and 'preservation'. That Derrida, in distinction, explicitly situates 'to lift up and to suppress', or 'elevation and replacement', as the 'double meaning' contained in *aufheben*,[18] amounts to *elevating*, as it were, the sense of 'elevation' itself, promoting it to a position of prominence denied it by Hegel. This reordering of conceptual components obviously draws on the dialogue with Hegelian idealism so central to Derrida's thought: one thinks notably of his defining *differance* as 'the limit, the interruption, the destruction of the Hegelian *relève wherever* it operates',[19] in terms of which the resolution/reappropriation of differences by *raising* them *up* to a higher spiritual sphere would be thwarted through its dis-solution within a non-totalizable series of referrals, such as might, in fact, be subversively enacted by Derrida's very translation of *auf*heben by *re*lèver were the French prefix seen to stress the effect of substitutive repetition rather than reconstitute a 'heightening' through its function as an intensifier. But, beyond this, it must be quite simply understood to yield a rendering of Hegel's term in French that is resolutely resonant with a movement of ascension.[20] Those who disregard this run the risk not only of misinterpreting/mistranslating Derrida himself,[21] but also of misapprehending the semantic network operative in others' appropriation of Derrida's Hegelian 'translation-interpretation'. In short, it is essential to grasp *relève/relever*'s elevated sense of elevation if we are to understand the inflexion proper to Badiou's technical use of the terms.

The choice to render *relève* and *relever* as 'raising up' and 'to raise up' in translating Badiou's *Second Manifesto* obviously draws on the considerations we've just mentioned. Yet, what primarily determined this choice is, and could only be, the particular characteristics imparted to these terms (or, if one prefers, to the dialectical process) within Badiou's own system of thought, where they figure as a crucial operator of his theory of the event – or, more precisely again, of what Badiou names 'the inexistent'. As an element that, while *in* a world, doesn't however appear in it, the inexistent can best be grasped intuitively by way of the example Badiou gives, following Marx's analyses, of the proletariat as the inexistent peculiar to political multiplicities. Certainly, there is no doubting the social and economic being of the proletariat, yet, in terms of the rules governing what appears in the political world, the proletariat simply *does not exist*. 'It is there but with a minimal degree of appearing, namely zero. [. . .] The proletariat is completely subtracted from the sphere of political presentation.'[22] It is, however, possible for the rules governing what appears in the world to undergo a radical change such that there occurs a fundamental (if, at first, very localized) reordering of the distribution of intensities of existence in the world. When such a reordering occurs, we can, in Badiou's terms, talk of an 'event'. That an event's modification of the system of rules governing appearing – a system Badiou names 'the transcendental' of a world – consists fundamentally in the 're-evaluation' of an inexistent, such as the proletariat as far as appearing politically is concerned, is, then, what we need to grasp: 'One sees this empirically in every true event: something whose value of existence in the world was nil or extremely weak all of a sudden, *eventally*, obtains a strong, indeed, maximal intensity of existence. The core of the question of the event, in appearing, is really: "We are nothing, let us be all", as sung in the *Internationale*. [. . .] An existence – the political existence of workers, for example – that had been measured by the transcendental as minimal, that is "nil" from the point of view of the world, suddenly proves to have a maximal measure.'[23]

From 'nothing' to 'all', from the degree 0 of existence to the maximal degree: this passage, or, more accurately, this veritable *upsurge*, is what Badiou qualifies as the *relève* – the 'raising up' – of an inexistent. There is, then, no doubting that this operation consists of an 'elevation' – indeed, on those occasions when Badiou proffers a synonym of the word *relève* in the *Second Manifesto* or elsewhere, the words he uses are: 'elevation', 'raising' (*levée*), 'insurrection', and even 'resurrection'.[24] Yet the raising up of the inexistent cannot be a matter of 'elevation' alone – as Badiou's very appropriation of the Hegelian concept (via Derrida's translation) attests. We need, therefore, to bring out the way in which it can equally be said to encompass – be this in strict fidelity to Hegel or not – the conjoined processes of suppression and preservation. To this end, several precisions of a more technical nature with respect to Badiou's concepts of existence and the event are in order. These will equally allow us to, then, set down the senses of 'raising up' and 'to raise up' that qualify them as translations conveying the evental operation that can be said to constitute, in more senses than one, the very core of the *Second Manifesto*'s reaffirmation of the existence of philosophy.

Without attempting to recapitulate the systematic intricacies of Badiou's definition of existence within the framework of the distinction between the ontological sphere of being qua being and the phenomenological sphere of appearance – a definition that forms the focus of much of the *Second Manifesto* as well as *Logics of Worlds* – suffice it to state here that a 'thing' or 'multiplicity' is said to appear when its elements are put into relation with others by what Badiou calls 'degrees of identity' (themselves organized in the 'transcendental system' already referred to), by means of which it is possible to both compare things with other things and to evaluate the differences and identities immanent to any given thing itself. The evaluation of a multiplicity's own elements yields, as such, a degree of identity that is assigned to the multiplicity in question, and it is this measure of a multiplicity's self-identity, understood as the intensity with which it appears in the field of relations constitutive of a 'world', that Badiou names 'existence'. Now, of the three characteristics by which Badiou defines an event in the *Second Manifesto* – power, intensity and reflexivity – the first pertains precisely to the 'raising up of the inexistent from the minimal or nil degree of existence to a maximal degree', attesting, as we've just seen, to the event's power of changing the very order of things. The second relates to the event's having itself a maximal degree of existence, while

the third, reflexivity, must be understood to constitute an *exception* to the protocol just outlined,
whereby a multiplicity's appearing is a function of
an immanent evaluation of the network of relations between its elements. In fact, in the case of
an event, a multiple (named a 'site' by Badiou)
itself falls under the general measurement of identities rendering possible the comparison of its
elements' appearing. Such an occurrence is a
singular transgression of the ontological-logical
complex that brings a multiple-being into appearing since, as the ontological support for things'
(or objects') appearing, a multiple-being does not
itself normally appear. Indeed, a fundamental law
of the mathematicity of Badiou's ontology (aligned
on the axioms of set theory) prohibits any multiple from entering into its own composition. In
the case of a site, however, the multiple 'belongs
to itself' (hence its 'reflexivity') such that its basis
in being comes, as Badiou puts it, 'to the surface
of its appearing "in person"'. In other words, 'a
being appears under the rule of the object whose
being it is'.[25] That such an occurrence is destined
to vanish almost as soon as it appears – for, as an
exception to the laws of being, it is incapable of
defying these for any length of time – means that

the raising up of the inexistent element alone preserves (at least initially) the *evental* value of the
site. Or put otherwise, the inexistent's attaining a
maximal intensity in the world of appearing is not
only that which strictly defines the site as an event
(for there are sites that do not qualify as events
through their failing to give rise to a consequence
of this magnitude), but it is also what '*now stands
in the place of* what has disappeared; its maximality is the *subsisting* mark of the event itself in the
world'.[26]

Both preserving and 'standing in the place of'
the pure vanishing of the 'insurrection of the
site', the raised-up inexistent would indeed, then,
result from a process that – were we to parasiti-
cally paraphrase Derrida's formulation cited previously – could be described as one in which a
multiple's (or site's) basis in being 'is both raised
up in its functions (by coming to the surface
of the appearing of the object whose being it
is) and relieved of them (thereupon to vanish),
replaced in a kind of promotion (the raising up
of the inexistent) by that which (the maximality
of the inexistent's appearing) follows or relays
or relieves it'. Yet we must immediately complement this formulation, seeking basically to simply

bring out the senses in which the raising up of the inexistent is a process conjoining preservation and replacement, by two precisions.

First, if the evental site can be said to be at the core of Badiou's dialectic of being and appearing, this is because its 'subversion of appearing by being' is dependent on its status as neither being nor non-being, neither appearing nor non-appearing – in short, on its constituting an *exception* to the laws proper to both these orders. This is brought out very clearly by Badiou in an interview that, focusing on the place of the dialectic within his philosophical enterprise, prompts him to specify that 'the category of exception is a dialectical one because the thinking of exception always takes place on two contradictory fronts. An exception must always be thought as a negation because it is not reducible to what is ordinary but nor can it be thought of as a miracle. It has to be thought as internal to the process of – non-miraculous – truth, but thought nonetheless as an exception.'[27]

Second, from its status as an exception within the ontological-logical complex governing the appearing of being, and, hence, as something both 'interior' to this complex but, at the same time, 'exterior to this "interiority"', it follows that the raising up of an inexistent (upon which, it should be noted, depends the formation of a truth) qualifies as a process of *negation*. For, to cite Badiou again, this torsion of interiority and exteriority constitutes 'the core of the dialectic': 'In Hegel, for example, the negation of a thing is immanent to this thing but, at the same time, it goes beyond this thing. The core of the dialectic is this status of negation, as an operator that at once separates and includes.'[28] With the raising up of an inexistent, something that *is* in the world but denied appearance there by the transcendental order dictating what can and cannot appear, suddenly comes – as an exception – to exist maximally, thus attesting to its 'separation' from the previously prevailing regime of intensities, now radically transformed. As a result, if, as Badiou states in the *Second Manifesto*, it is the case that, according to 'a materialist prescription of the type "appearing = being", *negation is, in the form of an element struck by inexistence*',[29] then it would seem equally possible to state, on the level of the determination making an event an exception to both being and appearing, that: *negation is, in the form of an inexistent raised up to maximal existence.*

Now, the fact that neither of the above formulations with respect to negation would be conceivable for Hegel indicates that Badiou's theory of the inexistent – entailing, as it does, that it is possible for a being *not* to appear at all – constitutes, in fact, a crucial locus at which Badiou's dialectic of being and appearing takes its distance from the dialectic's 'father'.[30] That admitted, however, the outline just given of the way in which the raising up of an inexistent encompasses, along with 'the motif of elevation', the conjoined processes of preservation and negation suffices here to bring out the constellation of conceptual coordinates that, constitutive of Badiou's technical use of the terms *relève* and *relever*, was determining for our choice of translation. To put this succinctly: in so far as it is by virtue of its very process of passing from a zero degree of existence to a maximal degree that an element both *preserves* the evental status of the site it comes to stand in the place of, on the one hand, and, attests to the operation of negation or, say, *suppression*, on the other, the sense that seemed to us paramount to capture in the translation of Badiou's technical use of *relève/relever* is, indeed, that of 'elevation'.

These considerations alone – independently,

in other words, of Badiou's explicit disapprobation of technical neologisms – dissuaded us from
translating his use of *relever* by the conventional
English-language rendering of Hegel's *aufheben,*
'to sublate'. At the same time, they obviously
confirm that the primary reason for our choosing
'to raise up', once the recourse to 'sublate' was
disqualified, lies in Badiou's own inflexion of
relever and not in Derrida's. Whatever the emphasis Derrida places on the theme of elevation,
this nevertheless remains, within the particular
torsion his texts give to *relever*, strictly insepara-
ble from that of replacement – which explains the
recourse to terms such as 'relay' or 'relieve' on the
part of his translators.[31] Of course, in translating
Badiou, the context on its own – without regard
to any analysis of conceptual complexity – ruled
out such renderings: in everyday language, the
operation of passing from a minimal value to a
maximal one is, clearly, not characterized as one
of replacement or of relief. Even if one could
argue such an operation to entail a sort of 'superior substitution', one obviously talks – in 'ordinary' mathematical parlance, for example – of
'raising a number to a given power', and not of
'relaying' or 'replacing' it.

That admitted, one might, though, query our adding the preposition 'up' to the verb. After all, not only does the mathematical usage just cited plead in favour of 'to raise' alone, but the desideratum of finding a word that, in addition to the motif of elevation, would contain the senses of 'preserve' and 'suppress' might similarly seem satisfied by the verb on its own. 'To raise a barrier', for example, can refer as much to a wall's being erected as to its being pulled down – as the locution 'raising a siege' brings out more immediately – or, yet again, to its being raised higher, such that the existing structure is preserved and augmented. This being the case, the semantic range covered by 'to raise' – which coincides, it should be noted, with virtually all the senses accruing to *relever* listed previously: to lift, to pull up, to restore, to enhance, etcetera – would, indeed, seem simply curtailed by the adjunction of the preposition, such that its equivalence to the French term would be restricted to the theme of elevation – or elevation/preservation – alone.

Here, as justification for our choice of 'raise up' and not 'raise' alone, we could contend that the preposition is required to capture the prefix 'auf' of *aufheben*, just as the verb (in conformity with *lever*) maintains the German stem's sense of 'to lift'. As such, it would then be but a matter of granting 'raise' to *actively* retain, despite the preposition, its values of 'preserve' and 'suppress' – in exactly the same way as, in the case of *relever*, the 'conjoined' meanings attributed to it only have *simultaneous* force in Derrida's speculative seizure of the term. Further, from a more pragmatic point of view, we could point out that the preposition does, indeed, seem called for, in so far as the 'raising up' of the inexistent element – in accordance, it should be noted, with its status as the 'result' of a dialectical process – always refers to the operation as *accomplished*: it is, after all, the *consequence* of an event. The preposition marks this perfective aspect of the operation, underscoring, as it were, what Badiou describes at one point in the *Second Manifesto*, as 'the heights of the authority' granted to the inexistent by 'its having been raised up'.[32] Yet, however legitimate such justifications might be, they are not – if we may put it this way – the most 'relevant', for the fact is that the English language includes a specific semantic instance of 'to raise up' that not only (unlike the case of 'to raise a barrier') *simultaneously* contains all three themes of 'to lift', 'to preserve' and 'to suppress', but also confirms it as a translation particularly apt to convey the eventual operation signified by *relever* in Badiou's inflexion of the term. As an illustration of the sense we are referring to here, imagine an incitation to revolt serving to 'raise a people up' in arms. As agents of an insurrection, 'the people' obviously preserve their identity, all while transmuting this into a self-constituted one that, in so far as it coincides with their now undeniably elevated, existential intensity, no less spells the end of their political subordination or 'subjective incapacity'.[33] The raising up of a people is, in short, at once the preservation of its identity, now elevated to a maximal degree of existence, and the suppression of (or separation from) the regime of appearing relegating it to subordination/inexistence. Elevation, preservation, suppression: that this threefold sense of 'raising up' leads us to rejoin Badiou's 'canonical' example of the raising up of the proletariat as an inexistent within the political world could, arguably, be construed as a certain speculative chance accruing to the English language. Such speculation aside, however, it is, incontestably, a felicitous concurrence on which to conclude a preface to the *Manifesto* that follows.

Acknowledgements

My thanks are due, first and foremost, to both Jennifer McCamley, whose meticulous scrutiny of the penultimate draft of this text helped fashion a far more fluid, final version, and Justin Clemens, for complementing his ever relevant comments on the translation with stimulating support in respect of various speculative interrogations. I would also like to express my gratitude to: Grant Cairns, Paul Giffard, Salim Oukrine and Eon Yorck, who all offered invaluable help on particular points of problematicity; Sarah Lambert, Helen Gray and Clare Ansell at Polity Press, whose professionalism and patience made it a pleasure to work with them; and Timothy Mathieson, for persevering with etymological substitutions to sublation, however misguidedly. Finally, I am indebted to Alain Badiou for having proposed that I undertake this translation and for countenancing my persistent queries throughout its elaboration.

Louise Burchill

0 Introduction

To write a Manifesto, even for something whose claim to intemporality is as powerful as philosophy's, is to announce that the moment has come to make a declaration. A Manifesto always comprises an 'it is time to say' that blurs any distinction between what it says and when it says it. What authorizes me, then, to judge that a Manifesto for philosophy is on the agenda, and a second Manifesto at that? What is thinking in our times?

That an intense philosophical 'moment' took place in France between the 1960s and 1980s – from the last great works of Sartre to the major texts of Althusser, Deleuze, Derrida, Foucault, Lacan, Lacoue-Labarthe or Lyotard, to mention simply the dead – must be unhesitatingly conceded to my friend Frédéric Worms.[1] Proof of this, 'by negative example' as the Chinese say, is the unremitting effort the coalition of a handful of

1

Introduction

media stars and thrill-seeking Sorbonne profes-
sors put into denying that anything at all occurred
all those years ago that was truly great – or even
just OK. This coalition has shown that it will stop
at nothing when it comes to imposing its sterile
condemnation upon public opinion. It does not
even balk at sacrificing a whole generation of
young people put before the detestable alternative of a savage careerism enhanced with a
sprinkling of Ethics, Democracy and, if necessary,
Piety, or the no less savage nihilism of short-lived
pleasures of the *no-future*[2] variety. The upshot of
this dogged determination is that, between the
heroic efforts of present-day youth to rediscover
a voice that carries and the thinned-out ranks of
survivors and inheritors of the great epoch,[3] there
is now in philosophy a gaping hole that discon-
certs our foreign friends. As regards France, only
the election of Sarkozy manages to surprise them
as much as does this decline of our intellectuals these last twenty years. In reality, what our
'American friends' are always too quick to forget
is that, while France has been the scene of some
grandiose displays of mass hysteria flanked by
powerful conceptual inventions, it has also been
that of a tenacious, servile and anti-Communard

2

reaction to which regiments of intellectuals have never failed to rally in the cause of propaganda.

'You French philosophers we loved so much, whatever became of you during the bleak period of the eighties – or, even more so, the nineties?', is the question we're insistently asked. Well, we were getting on with what had to be done in various places of shelter we'd put together with our own hands. Nonetheless, there are now more and more signs indicating, despite, or because of, the seemingly disastrous deterioration of France's historical, political and intellectual situation, that we old survivors – devoting our faithful labour to the discontented and informed assault of new generations – are about to rediscover a bit of space and light, and some open air.

I published my first *Manifesto for Philosophy*[4] in 1989. It wasn't a happy time, believe me! The burial of the post-May 1968 'red years' by interminable years of Mitterrand, the haughtiness of the 'new philosophers' and their humanitarian paratroopers, human rights combined with the right of intervention as the sole means of assistance, the full-bellied Western fortress giving moral lessons to those starving the world over, the collapse without glory of the USSR and

3

the consequent abeyance of the Communist hypothesis, the Chinese reversion to commercial genius, 'democracy' ubiquitously identified with the morose dictatorship of a narrow oligarchy of financiers, professional politicians and TV presenters, the cult of national, racial, sexual, religious and cultural identities seeking to undo the rights of the universal . . . Preserving, under these conditions, the optimism of thought, trying out new political formulas in close collaboration with workers from Africa, reinventing the category of truth, embarking on the paths of the Absolute by way of a totally revamped dialectic of structures' necessity and events' contingency, giving way on nothing . . .: What a task! It is to this labour that bore witness my first *Manifesto for Philosophy*, as succinct as it was lighthearted; this small book being as though the memoirs of thought jotted down underground.

Twenty years on, given the inertia of things, it's even worse of course – but every night ends with the promise of dawn. It would be difficult to stoop lower: on the level of state power than Sarkozy's government; on the level of the global situation than the bestial form taken by American militarism and its lackeys; on the level of the police than the countless controls, villainous laws, systematic brutalities, walls and barbed-wire fences uniquely aimed at protecting rich and self-satisfied Westerners from their natural, no less than innumerable, enemies – namely, the billions of destitute the world over, Africa above all; on the level of ideology than the miserable attempt at setting against so-called Islamic barbarians a secularism in rags and a comical 'democracy' capped off, for a tragic touch, by the disgusting exploitation of the Nazi extermination of the European Jews;[5] and, finally, on the level of knowledge than the strange concoction we're supposed to swallow of a technologized scientism, the crowning glory of which is the visualization of stereoscopic brains in colour, combined with a bureaucratic legalism whose supreme manifestation is the 'evaluation' of all things by experts hailing from nowhere who invariably conclude that thinking serves no purpose and even proves harmful. Nevertheless, however low we may have sunk, there are, I would repeat, signs serving to sustain the principal virtue of the moment: courage, in a form that rests largely upon the certainty of the imminent – indeed, already effective – return of the affirmative power of the Idea. This return is what the present book is dedicated to. The question around which it is structured is precisely: what is an Idea?

From the narrow point of view of my own work, I can obviously state that this *Second Manifesto for Philosophy* bears the same relation to the second volume of *Being and Event*, published in 2006 under the title *Logics of Worlds*,[6] that my first Manifesto bore to the first volume, published in 1988: it presents a simple and immediately mobilizable version of themes that the 'great work' painstakingly sets out in their full, formalized and exemplified form. From a broader perspective, however, it's just as possible to state that the aim of the short clarified version, in 1988, was to attest to the fact of thought's persevering underground, while, in 2008, it became that of showing there are perhaps the means of its resurfacing.

As such, it is probably not a coincidence that the central question of *Being and Event* in 1988 was that of the *being* of truths, thought in the concept of generic multiplicity, whereas in 2006, in *Logics of Worlds*, the question became that of truths' *appearing*, with this found in the concept of a body of truth or subjectivizable body.

Let us simplify, and let us hope: twenty years ago, writing a Manifesto amounted to saying: 'Philosophy is something completely different from what you are told it is. Try then to see what you are not seeing.' Today, writing a Manifesto is rather a matter of saying: 'Yes! Philosophy can be what you desire it to be. Try to really see what you are seeing.'

0.1 Outline

A Manifesto for philosophy philosophically declares, then, the existence of philosophy at a given moment of this existence. It does so according to rules that immanently command a declaration of existence, whatever this may be. Hence a requisite methodological order:

1. The necessity to philosophically declare the existence of philosophy ensues from opinion's doubting, or even, refuting this. What relevance would such a declaration have otherwise? Accordingly, we must begin with opinion such as it governs the moment when the declaration is necessary. What are opinion's themes, what are its operations and why, when all is said and done, does it entail a negation of philosophy's existence? Our first heading, then, will be: *Opinion*.

2. Since that in question is the existence of philosophy at the present moment and not its intemporal essence, the declaration must duly bear on

philosophy's *existence* in the world such as it is and not on its presumed transhistorical *being*. Existence is, however, a category of appearing in a determined world, whereas being is a category of that which constitutes any world regardless of its singularity. Concerned as it is with philosophy's existence here and now, the Manifesto must, as a result, explain what is meant by the appearing of any reality. Our second heading is necessarily then: *Appearance*.

3. Yet, if the appearing of that which is at issue in philosophy at the present moment is precisely what opinion denies, it is impossible for the appearing that we are concerned with (that commanding philosophy's existence) to be identified with appearing in general. Indeed, appearing 'in general' is precisely the reason opinion gives for its maintaining that nothing properly philosophical (as I understand it) does appear, is capable of appearing or should appear in the world such as it is and such as it will stay. As a result, the conceptual investigation on which the Manifesto rests focuses upon that which, differentiating appearance, marks out its forms and presents within it distinct, even contradictory, objects. In short, the logic of worlds should be thought of

as the difference of differences. Hence our third heading: *Differentiation.*

4. We cannot, however, confine ourselves to the logical regulation of differences, given that it is not simply philosophy's relation to what it is not that counts but philosophy's existence and, hence, its self-relation within the destiny determining whether it exists or disappears. We have to show the existential consistency of philosophy today and, in order to do so, we need philosophy's appearance to be identical to the force of its existence. What, though, is it to exist? This is our fourth question, which imposes the heading: *Existence.*

4.1. Once we have defined the category of existence, we'll apply this to the existence of philosophy, comparing its existence in the world today to that orchestrated by the world twenty years ago.

5. This is still not enough, however, to show that there is a particular philosophical *urgency,* which nothing in the presentation of the world puts on the agenda. That we philosophers can declare this to be the case, without this proving 'in general' to be very convincing, clearly indicates that our mapping of what exists in an

intense and urgent fashion – the legitimacy of our Manifesto being founded thereupon – is not the same as that laying down the law in the world such as this world appears. We must, then, maintain and rationally set out that there are moments such that a fundamental change affects that which organizes the way in which intensities of existence and urgencies of action are distributed. Something literally accedes to a maximal existence that had previously, to the minds of all, not existed, so to speak. The moment of the Manifesto is the moment when that by means of which philosophy is possible, as innovation and negation with regards to what appears, surges up in the context of a fundamental (albeit at first very localized) reordering of the distribution of intensities in the world such that 'something' appears in the world – something which demands philosophical attention and whose appearance is of such a nature that it can be said of this 'thing': 'it was nothing, now it is everything'. In short, every Manifesto claims there to be, on the scale of the world in which it makes its philosophical declaration, a sort of fine and implacable break in the laws governing appearing. This forces us to take as our fifth heading: *Mutation*.

6. We can reasonably give the name 'bodies' (I'm a materialist) to that which exists in a world. If the 'thing' of concern to philosophy surges forth in the world, it does so in the form of a body's becoming. What the Manifesto urges its readers to do, then, is to experiment with this body's existence in such a way that they become aware of why, with this utterly new existence, it is philosophy's reaffirmed existence that is at stake. Experimenting with the existence of a body is a practice, not a representation. It involves sharing its becoming, with all the vicissitudes the latter entails, and making of the individual that one is, perhaps along with millions of others, perhaps almost all alone, a component of this body's deployment in a world that had, but a short time before, judged it to be inexistent. Without doubt, it can be considered reasonable to call this an *Incorporation*.

7. Incorporation cannot be reduced to the purely objective dimension of an increased exist-ence of the new body, which is, all in all, a sort of glorious body.[1] What is really involved is the orientation of such a body, with this being what particularly calls for philosophy. What are we to understand by 'orientation'? The strictly subjective

question is what one subjects this body to in its intraworldly becoming. While its power can be displayed through a succession of tests and trials, its existence can also be limited, or even denied, from within its very becoming or, finally, it can be made merely the servile copy, or even the enemy, of a sacralized, extraworldly Body. One's incorporation can, in short, be positive, negative, or take the form of a counter-incorporation. Being a matter of how one conducts one's life with regard to whatever comes to pass, these variants of the relation between individuals and the new body are at the very core of philosophical examination. There can be no question of our naming them anything other than variants of *Subjectivation*.

8. The ultimate philosophical theme is that of the Idea, with this being understood as what organizes a subjectivation, such that individuals can picture themselves as giving impetus to the new body. This, put more simply, is the answer to philosophy's ultimate question: what is a life worthy of the name? The Manifesto reaffirms, under the conditions of the present, that philosophy can give an answer, or at least the form of an answer, to this question. The imperative of

the world, which is the imperative of short-lived pleasures, simply sets down: 'Live only for your satisfaction, and live, therefore, without Idea.' Against this abolition of life-thought, philosophy declares that to live is to act so that there is no longer any distinction between life and Idea. This indiscernibility of life and Idea is called: *Ideation*.

Accordingly, the Manifesto's declaration is divided into: Opinion, Appearance, Differentiation, Existence, Mutation, Incorporation, Subjectivation and Ideation.

After which will come the moment to conclude: to live 'as an Immortal', as the Ancients sought to, is, whatever one may say, within the reach of anyone.[2]

14

1 Opinion

It has become difficult to challenge opinion, even though this would seem the duty of all philosophy since Plato. Is it not, first of all, the immediate content of that which in our countries – by which I mean those whose State takes the form of parliamentary 'democracy' – is the most highly regarded freedom of all: the freedom of opinion? Second, is it not another name for what is polled and pampered and, if possible, purchased: namely, public opinion? After all, opinion polls have surely led to the coining of that most curious of clauses: 'the French think that', which is odd on at least two counts. For one thing, it is relatively certain that 'the French', not constituting in any way a Subject, are incapable of 'thinking' anything at all. For another, even assuming that the French comprise a coherent group, you would have to sum up the poll in terms of what it actually puts a figure to, and specify as a result:

'According to our latest figures, after elimination
of bias due directly to the stupid question put to
them, so many per cent of French people hold
such and such an opinion, so many per cent a
contrary opinion, and so many per cent no opinion at all.' Nevertheless – and this is the third
reason for the fetishism of opinion – far from
seeing the triplet of conformist opinion, anarchic
counter-opinion, and prudent non-opinion take
shape in reaction to a murky questionnaire, the
prevailing attitude considers these determinations
of opinion to be the necessary guide for public
action. Take the example of that indisputable
democrat, Michel Rocard, the socialist prime min-
ister whom Mitterrand delighted in keeping on a
tight leash and scolding every day. He had the
gift of superb political slogans, which his succes-
sors never tire of repeating. 'France cannot take
in all the wretched of the earth' is one example,
which has since assured the success of all the villainous laws against foreign workers. The slogan
that interests us here, no less set in the steel of
language, proposes to France and its leaders
another prohibition: 'One doesn't govern against
polls.' So much then for Plato's philosopher-king
and his obsession with the Just and True! Against

the authority of opinion, there is no possibility of 'good governance' – to use the ethical jargon in vogue. Opinion rules!

Basically, what all this going-on about opinion and its freedom, polling and authority comes down to, is that, as far as politics is concerned (though, ultimately, as we shall see, in all instances where thinking seems required), *no principle whatsoever should be advanced other than that proclaiming there are no principles.* The democrat will, moreover, happily add to this that holding to principles as though they were absolute is the very stuff of totalitarianism. 'Only fools don't change their minds' s/he will recall, with a kindly smile at your mental backwardness. S/he will cite as evidence the lightning speed with which the world changes, this alone sufficing to condemn the inflexibility of supposed principles: no sooner is a principle announced than it is already outdated! S/he will conclude that this is the reason why, moreover, there are only opportunistic rules for 'flexible management', on the one hand, and juridical rules to defend liberties from the obsession with principles, on the other. The freedom of entrepreneurship obviously has priority – 'setting up a business' or choosing one's bank come before all else, on the side of practical flexibility. Yet, immediately afterwards, on the juridical side, there is the freedom to hold any opinion one wants, unless this denies the right of others to different opinions. All is a matter of management and law: everything else but mere words.

'Damn!' exclaims the philosopher, overwhelmed by the prevailing attitudes. 'That's really impressive! Let's take a closer look.' And the philosopher then asks the democrat: if there are no principles, what is there by means of which the diversity of opinions relates to something real? Or, in what way is decision something other than being carried along by the current like a dead dog? What does your law without principles draw its authority from, and why is your flexible management most often a matter simply of going along with the play of forces? To use a little jargon: what is your ontology?

To this the democrat replies that there are, firstly, individuals with their opinions and the right to have them, and, secondly, communities or cultures with their customs and the right to them. Law regulates the *relations* between individuals and communities, while management

18

assures the *development* of communities for the greater advantage of individuals. The latter are, as such, assured harmony, the former growth, while both acquire harmonious growth and sustainable development.

Reeling from the blow of sustainable development, the philosopher can then but confess that, all argumentation aside, it is sadly impossible for him[1] to share such a view. As set down by Plato first of all, the axioms of philosophy cannot be those of 'the democrat', understood as the sophist – that is to say, precisely the proponent of the freedom of opinion, including the freedom of completely changing it.

That said, the philosopher will agree with the democrat that in a certain sense only individuals and communities can be said to exist. No God, no Angels, no Spirit of History, no Races, no Tables of Law . . . Fine. Individual multiplicities and complex cultures are all one deals with when it comes to existence. Yes, the philosopher today shares with the democrat (or the sophist – for, again, they are one and the same) this materialist postulate, which can be generalized as follows: 'There are only bodies and languages.' This maxim may be declared to be that of democratic materialism and the active core of dominant ideology. That a dominant ideology has to dominate is not contested by the philosopher whose consent on this point does not spare himself: he too, the philosopher, is dominated by democratic materialism. Broadly, then, there only exists what the axiom of democratic materialism states exists: bodies and languages.

This is the case in broad terms only, however, for on an extremely detailed level there are exceptions. There equally exist 'things' – let us remain vague for the moment – that cannot be identified with either individual singularities or cultural constructions. Such 'things' are immediately universal in the sense that they possess a value – a sort of particular resistance – that can be appropriated by another world, another culture and other individuals than the world, culture or individuals that participated in their emergence and development, and this despite what there is foreign about the bodies and languages making up their materiality. In short, this kind of 'thing' functions in a transworldly fashion, with 'world' here being understood as a materialist totality made up of bodies and languages. Created in one world, it is valid *actually* for other worlds and *virtually* for all. It is, we might say, a supplementary possibility – since it cannot be deduced solely from the material resources of the world which appropriates it – that is available to all.

Certainly, such a 'thing' is materially composed of bodies and languages. It is, to put this simply, created by given individuals in given cultures. Yet its process of creation is of such a nature that it can be understood and used in individual and symbolic contexts that are as vastly distant as they are different, in space as in time.

This kind of 'thing' can be: art (the Chauvet cave paintings, Wagner's operas, Lady Murasaki's novels, the Easter Island statues, Dogon masks, Balinese choreographies, Indian poems . . .); or science (Greek geometry, Arabic algebra, Galilean physics, Darwinism . . .); or politics (the invention of democracy in Greece, the peasant movement in Germany at the time of Luther, the French Revolution, Soviet Communism, the Chinese Cultural Revolution . . .); or of the order of love (everywhere, innumerable). Are there yet other things, other types of things? Perhaps. I do not know of any but would be happy, if these things exist, to let myself be convinced of their existence.[2]

Taking the form of sciences, arts, politics and loves, these 'things', endowed with a transworldly and universal value, are what I name *truths*. The whole point – which is, moreover, extremely difficult to think through and which will take up almost all the rest of this book – is that *truths exist* just as do bodies and languages. Hence the exception that the philosopher has to introduce into the dominant context of democratic materialism.[3]

Indeed, truths do not constitute an *objection* to democratic materialism but an *exception* to it. We propose, therefore, to formulate the philosophical maxim, which is both internal and external – or, as Lacan would have put it, 'extimate' – to the protocol of democratic materialism, as follows: *there are only bodies and languages except that there are truths.*

Obviously, this slight transformation changes the status of opinion. We may state opinion to be what can be said of bodies or languages in a given language, as soon as *bodies and languages are grasped in the same world*. A truth can never, then, be reduced to an opinion because it has a transworldly value, such that it can only be appropriated by being grasped, not *in the same world*, but in accepting a certain – and often considerable – *indifference to the particular world* or, what comes to the same thing, a certain *affirmation of the unity of worlds once these are considered from the point of view of truths.*

Everything hinges on the fact that, although created in a particular world with materials (bodies and languages) of this world, truths are not principally marked as belonging to this specific world and, as a result, convey with them the possibility that worlds differing in other aspects are, nevertheless, 'the same' from the point of view of the truths in question.

Marx asked how is it that, in our industrial world, we are so moved by Greek myths when Zeus' lightning bolts pale into insignificance next to the potency of a power station. His response – that the Greek world represents our childhood and that there is something charming about childhood per se – is as feeble as it is touching. We might add that this origin story is also very German. In fact, the question is badly posed. One should not start off from the difference of worlds – the archaic versus the industrial – and then set up as enigmatic what they have in common (a tragedy by Sophocles, for instance). Rather, one should start with truths, with these thereby affording the insight that, from the standpoint of Sophocles' tragedy, the two worlds can, in reality, just as well be viewed as the same.

Truths, and truths alone, unify worlds. They transfix the disparate composites of bodies and languages in such a way that, for a split second or sometimes longer, these are, as it were, welded together. This is why all truths introduce, within the play of established opinions, a sudden *change of scale*. That which is One in terms of mundane closure attains, through the welding of worlds, a vastly superior unity.

Against the democrat, the philosopher raises the objection of truths' exception as a change of scale as regards thought. Opinion is limited, its freedom consisting usually of the right to repeat that which holds sway, the law of the world. Only a truth opens the world to the One of an over-world, which is also the world-to-come, but such as this already exists in the guise of the True.

This equally shows that, if the democratic norm of opinion is freedom within the arena of its limitation, the thinking and philosophizing norm of truths is equality in the arena of illimitation. For, faced with a truth as when faced with a theorem, it is possible to say that while no one is really free, nor is anyone excluded. Yet one can equally say that whosoever places themselves in such a relation is free – this, though, being a matter of that new freedom which unfurls at the level of all worlds and not of one alone.

It is for this reason that, contrary to the opinion of the common democrat, there are well and truly principles. We will signal some of these later on for they can only be set out according to specific truths and not from a formal point of view. There are mathematical principles, or musical principles, amorous principles, or revolutionary ones . . . Philosophy, however, formulates a sort of principle of principles: *in order to think, always take as your starting point the restrictive exception of truths and not the freedom of opinion.*

This is a worker's principle in the sense that thought here is a matter of labour and not of self-expression. Process, production, constraint and discipline are what it seeks; not nonchalant consent to what a world proposes.

The philosopher is a worker in another sense: detecting, presenting and associating the truths of his or her time, reviving those that have been forgotten and denouncing inert opinion, s/he is the welder of separate worlds.

2 Appearance

That truths exist, be it as exceptions to the particular laws of a world, in no way exempts us from respecting our materialist axiom: in so far as everything that exists is woven out of bodies and languages, we must be able to explain how truths come to exist as bodies within a given world. We must, in short, be capable of thinking how truths *appear*.

I am a sophisticated Platonist, not a vulgar one. I do not uphold that truths pre-exist in a separate 'intelligible place' before becoming mundane and that they are born simply by descending from the heavens above. Certainly, a truth is eternal in that it is never confined to a particular time – such a restriction being hardly tolerable for that which is a prisoner of no world, not even that in which it is born. Any given time is always the time of a world. This, as we have seen, is what misled Marx himself: Sophocles' tragedy touches us not, as he claimed, because of its belonging to a previous bygone age but, rather, only inasmuch as its significance is not exhausted by that which materially binds it to its world of appearance. This is why, moreover, the 'cultural' presentation of art works so in vogue today, with its painstaking reconstitution of context, obsession with History and relativization of hierarchies of value, is ultimately so deadening: it operates on behalf of *our* conception of time (the historical and relativistic conception of democratic materialism) against the eternity of truths. Far preferable in this respect is the bric-a-brac of anarchic collections such as one used to see in small provincial museums, or the vertiginous shock of analogies (the angel of Reims brushing shoulders with a Khmer goddess) of the kind composing Malraux's 'imaginary museum'.[1] Yet the eternity of truths must be compatible with the singularity of their appearance. Descartes famously affirmed God to have created eternal truths. Our paradox is even more radical: created without any God, out of the particular materials of a world, truths are nonetheless eternal. We must, therefore, rationally account for nothing less than the appearance of eternity in time.

Appearance

Our starting point is, of course, a general doctrine of appearance.

In *Being and Event,* as in my first Manifesto, I showed that when the 'there is' is divested of all the qualitative predicates which make of it a singular thing (or what we will later call an object) and is reduced to its mere being, it may be thought of as a pure multiplicity. This tree that is in front of me will accordingly – should I strive to subtract, first, its effective presence in a specific world (its surroundings, the horizon, the other trees, the nearby meadow, etc.) and, then, the entanglement of determinations which make it cohere before me as a tree (the colour green, the spread of its branches, the play of light and shadow among its leaves, etc.) – end up reduced to an infinitely complex multiplicity composed of other multiplicities. No primordial, or atomic, unity will put a halt to this composition. The tree as such is not made up of tree atoms that would found its qualitative essence. What one comes upon at the end is not the One but the void. The tree is a particular interweaving of multiplicities which are themselves woven out of the void alone, in accordance with formal generative processes that only mathematics accounts for. Such was the pivotal thesis of the ontology I proposed twenty years ago: being is a multiplicity plucked from the void and the theory of being qua being is nothing other than mathematics. Which is quite simply to say that ontology, in its etymological sense of a discourse on being, is historically accomplished as a mathematics of multiplicities.

As a result, in the case of the tree – as in Valéry's poem for instance:

> You lean, great plane tree, offering yourself up
>   nude
> Like a Scythian youth, and just as white.
> But your candour is bound and your foot
>   secured
> By the force of the site.[2]

– it is not a question of that which is (mathematically) conceivable as the pure form of the tree's being. What's at issue is something altogether different: namely, this being as it appears in the world or constitutes, by its appearance, a component of the latter. The poem is not the guardian of being, as Heidegger thought, but the *exposure* to language of the resources of appearing. Further, this exposure itself is not yet the *thinking* of

29

appearing, which, as we will see, takes the form of *logic* alone.

Let us take any multiplicity. That this multiplicity appears means simply that, in addition to its being qua being, which is intrinsically determined as a pure multiplicity (or multiplicity 'without One' because there are no atoms of being), there is the fact that this multiplicity is *there*. Hegel was right to join a doctrine of being-there to his doctrine of pure being. The fact that a multiple is in some way localized, such that the multiple-indifference of its being is assigned to a world, goes beyond the resource of this multiple-being as thought by mathematics. A sort of impetus, topological in essence, prevents the multiple from being merely what it is since, as what appears, it is *there* that it has to be what it is. But what is the meaning of this 'being there', this being that comes to be in so far as it appears? We do not have the means to separate an extension from what occupies it, or a world from the objects of which it is composed. Being qua being is absolutely homogeneous: a mathematically thinkable, pure multiplicity. There is not the localizing being of worlds and the localized being of objects. Nor is there the Universe as the absolute place of all there is. It is mathematically demonstrable that the theme of a *total* multiplicity or Multiplicity of all multiplicities is incoherent, which means that, being unthinkable, it is equally incapable of giving rise to a being – for Parmenides is right: being and thinking are the Same.

The result of all this is that the pure essence of being-there, or appearing, consists not of a form of being but of *forms of relation*. Our plane tree appears as such in so far as its pure being (a multiplicity) is differentiated from the plane tree next to it, the meadow, the red roof of the house, the black crow perched on a branch, etc. But it is also differentiated from itself when it 'leans' in the wind and shakes its foliage as a lion does its mane, thereby modifying its overall aspect even though it is also still the same as 'secured by the force of the site'. The world in which the plane tree appears is, therefore, for each multiplicity that figures within it, the general system of differences and identities that connects it to all the others.

One can reasonably call 'logic' a formal theory of relations. It follows that the thought of appearing is a logic. It is even possible to maintain that saying a thing 'appears' or saying it is 'constituted in a logic' comes to the same thing. The world in which the thing appears is this very logic as this is deployed with respect to all the multiplicities that figure within it.

The technical form of this logic will be rendered a bit clearer in the next chapter. What is essential to grasp here is that a truth, in so far as it appears, is a singular body that enters into a differentiating relation with an infinity of other bodies according to the rules of a logic of relation.

The process of a truth that appears in a world necessarily takes the form of a logical incorporation.

3 Differentiation

To think how a body of truth or subjectivizable body differs from an ordinary body, and, accordingly, how a truth's appearing differs from the appearing, as an object of a world, of any ordinary multiplicity, it is necessary to firmly grasp the protocols of differentiation that make up the logical identity of this world. Since appearing is the capture of multiples ontologically defined on the basis of the void by a network of differences and identities, it must be possible to define an intramundane singularity, such as a truth process, in terms of purely logical criteria internal to the formal system which regulates differences or, more generally, relations between multiplicities.

In order to arrive at this definition controlling what it means that truths *exist*, let us attempt to represent the situation of a world.

As given in their pure being, the multiplicities that coexist in this world can be drawn as circles of

Differentiation

various sizes (a quick glance at *Schema 1*, found on the inside flap of this book's cover, is advised for what follows). The notion of 'size' is very approximate here because any two multiplicities differ as soon as an element possessed by one of them is not an element of the other. As such, two multiplicities can very well be ontologically different even though they have the same 'size', that is, the same 'number' of elements. All it takes is for the multiplicities to differ on one point alone, as when they have the same elements except that α belongs to one and not the other, while the latter possesses β which is not in the first. That α is different from β suffices in itself for the two multiplicities to be absolutely different. This local – or, in other terms, extensional – dimension of difference makes it impossible to account for the difference between two multiples in sheer quantitative terms. That said, let us suppose that different circles represent different multiplicities – by which I mean *ontologically* different ones. This is a crucial and delicate point: ontological difference does not necessarily coincide with difference in appearing. This is why a plane tree by the side of a road undoubtedly differs from the one next to it, yet, to the eyes of a traveller in a hurry,

34

all the trees blur into one monotonous series where everything is the same. The trees appear to be overwhelmingly *similar* even though they are absolutely *different*. Within the register of appearing, they repeat the same pattern, whereas their multiple-being repeats nothing at all since any difference, even that attested to at a single point, is ontologically absolute. Were we to scale the world, on the contrary, to the field of vision of an individual reclining in a meadow between two plane trees and focused on the fine lacework of the leaves against the blue sky or the twisting of the upper branches, it is clear that the two plane trees would appear as what they are: essentially different. As a result, it is just as possible for that which holds for being qua being to equally hold for being-there as it is for the evaluation of differences in appearing to have nothing to do with the evaluation governing the basis in being of this appearing. The relation between 'being' and 'appearing' (or existing) is contingent. Genuine Platonism has never affirmed anything else, but this can in no way be taken to mean, as the attacks on vulgar Platonism assume, that appearing is of the order of falsehood or illusion. The difference between being and appearing is much

rather that which distinguishes mathematics (as
ontology) from logic (as phenomenology) – each
of these two disciplines being just as formalized
and rigorous as the other.

Let us carry on, however, with our exegesis
of schema 1. We will represent the logical frame
of the world by a plane beneath the circles. This
frame 'contains' special elements that we will
name *degrees*. Given two elements of a multiplicity (represented by two points in a circle), there
is a degree in the plane that corresponds to them.
This degree is that of the identity of the two points.
For instance, let us suppose that one of the circles
is the multiple of plane trees by the roadside.
Corresponding to two of the trees in the monotonous series imposed upon these by the road,
there is a degree of identity – let's say, degree
p. In so far as they appear in the world, these
two trees can then be said to be 'identical to the
degree *p*'. We have seen that this degree can be
very high if the world and its logic is that of the
weary motorist, who, by dint of seeing the trees
file past, confounds one with the other. The trees
all merge together as 'plane trees and more plane
trees'. As a result, the trees are strongly identical even if, ontologically, they are absolutely

different. An absolute ontological difference can appear in the logic of the world under the form of a quasi-identity. For the daydreamer reclining between two trees, scrutinizing their shapes and shades, the two trees are, on the contrary, clearly very different, such that the degree p of their identity is very weak. In this instance, the ontological difference appears under the form of a weak degree of identity and is, as a result, more in harmony with the underlying structure of being.

We are beginning to see that the degrees of identity that inscribe – as they alone do – multiplicities within the fabric of relations comprising a world, obey specific rules. For example, a principle of comparison between certain degrees must be able to exist for us to be able to say that two multiplicities that appear in a world, and whose identity is measured by a degree, are 'very identical' or, on the contrary, 'very different'. For this amounts to saying, in fact, that the degree p measuring the identity of the first two multiples is clearly 'larger' than the degree that measures the identity of the last two. So it is with the two plane trees caught in the headlights of the motorist in a hurry and those observed in minute detail by the daydreamer in the valley.[1] If the first two are identical to the degree p and the other two to the degree q, we have just explained that it must be possible to state that p is clearly greater than q. The conclusion being that *the structure of degrees is, essentially, an order structure.*

It is also clear that the reason two multiples appear to be completely different is because their degree of identity, in the world concerned, is practically nil. For this to have any sense, however, there obviously has to exist a degree which 'marks' this nullity and, hence, a degree smaller than all the others, which lays down a minimal identity of two multiples – with this implying, relative to the logic of the world concerned, an absolute difference, as is the case with the two trees under which lies our half-asleep dreamer. Inversely, if two multiples appear to be completely identical even though ontologically different, then their degree of identity is maximal, or larger than all the others. This requires such a degree to exist. In short, *the order structure of degrees admits a maximum and a minimum.*

A careful examination of the logical conditions of appearing, or being-there, shows that degrees of identity obey two further rules which I won't go into here but which are amply demonstrated, analysed and exemplified in Books II and III of *Logics of Worlds*. They deal, respectively, with the existence of the conjunction of two degrees and the existence of the envelope of an infinite set of degrees. It follows from these rules that the space of degrees, constitutive of the logic of a world, has the general structure of a Heyting algebra,[2] aptly named a 'locale'.[3] This name is apt because it is, indeed, a matter of the localization of the multiples of which every being is composed – the 'there' of being.

There exist many structures of this type that are not isomorphic. This diverse group is caught up in a tension between algebra and topology – between the theory of *operations* and that of *localizations* – which I have long believed to be at the core of all dialectical thought.[4] Let's say that this takes the following form here: the structure of degrees of identity that governs appearing can either belong to the 'classic' category of Boolean algebras or be much more clearly akin to the open sets of a topological space. In the first case, appearing obeys, via the measurement of degrees of identity, ordinary logic with the law of excluded middle, as is also the case of being as such, which, as we know since Parmenides, does not tolerate a third term between being and non-being. In the second case, an intuitionist logic without excluded middle generally proves to be that which constrains being-there to depart from the laws of pure being.

Beyond the fascinating details of the logic – or, rather, the *logics* – of appearing, what matters to us here is that its seeming infinite complexity is exhausted by the simple means of laws governing identities and differences. Order, maximum and minimum, conjunction and envelope are all that is needed for the difference between being and being-there to be thought. I've proposed that the system of these rules be called *transcendental*. In schema 1, the cross-section where all the local differences are indexed to degrees of identity represents the transcendental of the world. As with Kant's insight – taken up by Husserl – the transcendental is essentially a logical theme. The error, however, was to oppose transcendental logic to formal logic. For the logic of worlds is extracted, from start to finish, from certain inflexions of formal logic.

Heidegger famously aligned the destiny of metaphysics with a miscomprehension of ontological difference, thought as the difference between being and beings. If we interpret beings as the 'there' of being, or as the mundane localization of a pure multiple, or again, as the appearing of multiple-being – which is entirely possible – then that which is in question in what Heidegger calls ontological difference can be said to be the immanent gap between mathematics and logic. It would be proper then, in order to continue to follow him, to call 'metaphysical' any orientation of thought confusing mathematics and logic under the same Idea. Now, there are two ways of perpetrating this confusion. Either one reduces mathematics to a simple logical theory, which is what Frege, Russell and Wittgenstein[5] all do in their own manner. Or one considers logic to be but a specialized branch of mathematics, as many modern positivists do. As such, two meta-physics can be said to exist: the first dissolving being within appearing; the second denying that appearing is distinct from being. It is easy to recognize empiricism's variants in the first, dogmatism's variants in the second.

Philosophy only exists on condition that it stands firm on the dual consistency of being and being-there, the dual rationality of being qua being and appearing, and the intrinsic value and separation of mathematics and logic. On its two borders, moralizing empiricism and dogmatic theology, there has always been the stirring of aggressive phantoms. Here I am making the Manifesto of contemporary methods for their exorcism.

4 Existence

One of philosophy's fundamental problems since its inception has been to distinguish between *being* – which Aristotle was the first to seek to think *'qua being'* – and *existence*, qua a category that is precisely irreducible to the category of being. It is not exaggerated to say that the elaboration of this difference still dictates the destiny of a philosophical construction today.

What is meant by the word 'existence' frequently depends upon taking into consideration a special *type of being*. This is the case for Heidegger when he distinguishes between *Sein* and *Dasein*. From a strictly etymological point of view, 'existence' – which depends on *Dasein* – can be observed to be a topological concept. It signifies being there, being in the world. That the broad concept of existence necessarily entails thinking the place, the world, where every thing comes to be or, rather, to exist its being, is a determination that we obviously have to grant to Heidegger in the context of appearing as I define it. The inability to deduce this place from being as such is what founds the difference of *Sein/Dasein* or being/being-there. Yet, for Heidegger, 'Dasein' – and, ultimately, 'existence' – is a name for 'human reality', the historical destiny of thought and the crucial, creative experience of the becoming of being itself. I am going to propose, on the other hand, a concept of being-there and of existence without making the slightest reference to anything like consciousness, experience or human reality. From this point of view, I remain in the anti-humanist lineage of Althusser, Foucault or Lacan. 'Existence' is not a specific predicate of the human animal.

In Sartre's work, the distance between being and existence is a dialectical consequence of the difference between being and nothingness. In fact, existence is the effect of nothingness within the ambit of the full, stupid massiveness of being qua being, and designates the complex relation between being-in-itself, which is consumed entirely in being without ek-sisting or going-outside-itself, and being-for-itself, which differs from itself by nihilating the in-itself it potentially risks being. For my part, equally, the determination of the concept of existence is conditioned by something like negation as well as self-differing. Ontologically, this is, for me, the question of the void – the empty set. Phenomenologically, it is the question of negation in the various senses this can take in (classical, intuitionist and paraconsistent) logic and as applicable to the appearing of a multiple if one measures the degree of identity between this and its negation in a world. But I will plot these connections without any relation whatsoever with the conscious subject, and even less again with freedom. 'Existence' is not a specific predicate of the free subject or moral action.

As has been seen, my thought of being-there borrows something from Kant: namely, the fact that the appearing of a multiplicity presupposes the notion of a degree or intensity that measures the explicit relations between this multiplicity and all that co-appears in the same world. This idea is found in the famous passage of the first *Critique*, dealing with the anticipations of perception. But I am also going to borrow something from Hegel – namely, that existence must be thought as the movement that goes from pure being to being-there, or from essence to the phenomenon or appearing, as explained in two profound and obscure chapters of his *Logic*. That said, I shall strive to bring to bear this limited array of loyalties (Heidegger, Sartre, Kant and Hegel) without appealing to anything of the order of a historical notion of Being, transparent consciousness, transcendental subject or becoming of the Absolute Idea.

This will equally allow me to recapitulate the steps we have taken so far.

Let us set off from the question 'What is a thing?' This is the title of a famous essay by Heidegger.[1] What is a thing qua a 'there is' without any determination of its being, except precisely its being qua being? We can speak of an object of the world. We can distinguish it in the world by its properties or predicates. In fact, we can experiment with the complex network of identities and differences that render this object manifestly nonidentical to another object of the same world. But a thing is not an object. A thing is *not yet* an object. Like the hero of Robert Musil's great novel, a thing is something 'without qualities'. We need to think a thing *before* its objectivation in a specific world.

The thing is *das Ding*, even perhaps *das*

Ur-Ding – which is to say, that form of being that, while certainly situated after the indifference of nothingness, is nonetheless, equally, before the qualitative difference of the object. We must, then, formalize the concept of 'thing' between the absolute priority of nothingness (the void out of which all multiplicities are woven), on the one hand, and the complexity of objects, on the other. A thing is always the pre-objective basis of objectivity. This is the reason why a thing is nothing other than a multiplicity. Not a multiplicity of objects, not a system of qualities or network of differences, but a multiplicity of multiplicities, and a multiplicity of multiplicities of multiplicities. And so on. Is there an end to this type of 'dissemination', as Jacques Derrida would have put it? Yes, there is an endpoint. But this endpoint is not a primitive object or an atomic component; it is not a form of the One. The endpoint is also, necessarily, a multiplicity. This multiplicity is the multiplicity of no multiplicity – the thing which is also nothing, the void, the empty multiplicity, the empty set. The reason a thing is between indifference and difference, nothingness and objectivity, is because a pure multiplicity is composed of the void. The multiple as such has to do with difference and pre-objectivity. The void has to do with indifference and the total absence of any object.

Since the work of Cantor at the end of the nineteenth century, we have known that it is perfectly rational to propose this type of construction of pure multiplicities starting from the void as the framework for mathematics. This is the origin and justification of the thesis I evoked above, according to which, if ontology is the science of the thing, of the pure 'something', then we must conclude that ontology is mathematics. The thing is formalized as a set; the elements of this set are sets; and the starting point for the entire construction is the empty set.

It is at this point, on the path leading to existence, that the problem arises for us of understanding how objectivity originates. How can a pure multiplicity (a set) appear in a world, in a highly complex network of differences, identities, qualities, intensities and so on?

It is impossible to deduce something of this kind from the mathematical theory of multiplicities as sets of sets, composed ultimately of the pure void. If ontology, as the theory of things without qualities, is mathematics, then phenomenology, as the theory of appearing and objectivity, concerns the relation between qualitative differences or problems of identities, and this is where we encounter problems of existence. All of this requires thinking a place for appearing, or for being-there – a place that we call a world and which, for its part, does not exist given it is the condition of all existence.

After the mathematics of being qua being, we have set about developing, in our previous chapters, the logic of worlds. Unlike the logic of things, which are composed of sets of sets, it is impossible for the logic of worlds to be purely extensional. This logic must be that of the distribution of intensities within the field in which multiplicities are not merely limited to being but equally appear, there, in a world. The law of things is to be qua pure multiplicities (as things) but, equally, to be there qua appearing (as objects). The rational science pertaining to the first point is ontology, historically unfolded as mathematics. The rational science of the second point is logical phenomenology, in a much more Hegelian than Husserlian sense. Against Kant, we must maintain that we know being qua being, just as we no less know the way in which the thing-in-itself appears in a world. The Mathematics of multiplicities and the Logic of worlds designate, were we to adopt Kant's terminology, our first two 'critiques'. The third critique consists of the theory of the event, truth and the subject, an outline of which is given in this book from chapter 5 onwards, and is what any contemporary philosophy worthy of the name takes as its veritable goal – to answer the question: how are we to live, such that our life measures up to the Idea? In all of this, existence is a general category of the logic of appearing, belonging to the second critique, and can be discussed independently of any consideration of subjectivity. At this stage of our argument, 'existence' is to remain an a-subjective concept.

Suppose we have a pure multiplicity, a thing, which can be formalized as a multiple or set. We want to understand what exactly the appearing, or being-there, of this thing in a given world is. According to the idea set out in chapters 2 and 3, when the thing (the set) is localized in a world, this is because the elements of the set are inscribed within a completely new evaluation of their identities. It becomes possible to state that such and such an element, for example x, is more or less identical to another element, for example

y. In classical ontology, there are only two possibilities: either x is the same as y, or it is not at all identical to y. You have either strict identity or difference. Inversely, in a concrete world, as the place of multiplicities' being-there, we have a great variety of possibilities. A thing can be very similar to another, or similar in certain points and different by way of others, or somewhat identical, or very identical but not entirely the same, and so on. As a result, any element of a thing can be put into relation with others by what we call a degree of identity. The fundamental characteristic of a world is the distribution of this type of degree over all the differences that appear in this world.

Accordingly, the concept of appearing, or being-there, or world, itself possesses two characteristics. First, there must be a system of degrees, with an elementary structure rendering the comparison of degrees possible. We must be capable of observing if a given thing is more identical to such and such another than to a third. For this reason, degrees evidently have the formal structure of an order. They admit, perhaps within the compass of certain limits, 'more' and 'less'. This structure is the rational disposition of the infinite hues of a concrete world. I would recall that I have named this organization of degrees of identity the *transcendental* of a world. As for the second characteristic, this consists of a relation between things (multiplicities) and degrees of identity – which is, precisely, the meaning of 'being-in-a-world' for a thing. Once equipped with these two determinations, we would, then, have the signification of the becoming-object of the thing, followed by that of its existence.

Let us repeat the construction of what we will, from now on, call an object – namely, a multiple associated with an evaluation of the identities and differences immanent to it. Suppose we have a couple of elements of a multiple that appears in a world. To these elements there corresponds a degree of identity, such that this expresses the 'more' or 'less' identity between the two elements of this world. As a result, a degree in the transcendental of the world will correspond to any two elements. We name this relation an *identity function*. Such an identity function, operative between certain multiplicities and the transcendental of the world, is, in fact, the fundamental concept of the logic of being-there or appearing. If a pure multiplicity is a thing, a multiplicity accompanied by its degree of identity is an object (of the world).

Thus, the complete logic of objectivity consists in the study, on the one hand, of the form of the transcendental as a structural order and, on the other, of the identity function between multiplicities and the transcendental. Formally consisting in the study of types of structural order, the study of the transcendental is a technical issue involving formal fragments of a mathematical-logical nature in interplay with a fundamental philosophical intuition. As for the study of the identity function, this comes down to examining an important philosophical problem – namely, that of the relation between things and objects, or, in other words, between indifferent multiplicities and their concrete being-there. Here, I would simply like to consider three points.

First, it is very important to keep in mind that there are many types of orders and, consequently, many possibilities for the logical organization of a world. We must assume the existence of an infinity of different worlds, not simply on an ontological level (a multiplicity, a thing, is in a world and not another) but equally on a logical level – that of appearing and, thereby also, as we will see, of existence. Two worlds with the same things can be absolutely different from each other because their transcendentals are different. That is, the identities between the elements of the same multiplicity can radically differ on the level of their being-there in a world or in another.

Second, as we have seen, there is always in a world a certain number of limits to appearing's intensity. A degree of identity between two elements varies between two limit cases such that the two elements can be 'absolutely' identical or practically indiscernible within the logical framework of a world, or they can be absolutely nonidentical, absolutely different from each other, with no point in common. Between these two limits, the identity function can express the fact that the two elements are neither absolutely identical nor absolutely different. This idea is easily formalized. In a transcendental order, you have a minimal degree and a maximal degree of identity. Most often, you have a great number of intermediary degrees. When the identity function for a couple of elements in a world takes the maximal value, the two elements will be said to be absolutely identical in this world or to have the same appearing, the same being-there. When the identity function takes the minimal value, the two elements will be said to be absolutely different from each other, while, in the case of an identity function taking an intermediary value, the two elements will be said to be identical to a certain extent – with this extent indicated by this intermediary transcendental degree.

Third, in addition to its order, encompassing its maximum and minimum, a transcendental has structural laws that we can think by the means of logic and which lead us to speak in a more precise manner of an object's global determinations. We can, for example, examine the intensity of the being-there of a *part* of the world, even if this is infinite, rather than that of just a few elements. Or we can develop a theory of the smallest parts of an object, which I name *atoms of appearing*. An absolutely crucial principle comes into play in this theory, which I name the *fundamental principle of materialism*. The statement of this principle is very simple: 'any atom of appearing is real'. This indicates that at the atomic level – that is, when what is involved is a single element of the multiple that appears – the atom of appearing can be identified with a real element of the multiple in question (in the ontological sense: this element 'belongs' to it). We are engaged here in the most profound reflections on the connection between ontology and logic, between being and appearing. By adopting the principle of materialism, we admit that at appearing's minimal point there is a sort of 'fusion' with the being that appears. An atom of appearing is in a certain way 'prescribed' by a real element of the multiple.

Unfortunately, while the principle is simple to state, its formalization and rigorous examination exceed the scope of our Manifesto. What is to be kept in mind, however, is that any authentic philosophy of appearing is declared here to be materialist in the sense of this principle. In my first Manifesto, I wrote that philosophy, reuniting with the theme of Truth, must assume a 'Platonic gesture'. The second Manifesto declares that what is now on the agenda, with all its requisite conceptual rigour, is a Platonic materialism which will be seen later on to be a materialism of the Idea.

We have, then, an extensive and demanding comprehension of what happens to a multiplicity when it really appears in a world or when it is not simply reducible to its pure immanent composition. Multiplicities that appear must be understood as highly complex networks of degrees of identity between their elements, parts and atoms. This is what, in *Logics of Worlds*, I name 'atomic logic' and it forms the most subtle part of the theory of appearing. It demands an attention to the logic of qualities and not solely to the mathematicity of extensions. Beyond pure multiple-being, we have to think something like an 'existential intensity'.

This brings us to the point we wanted to get to: how do we set about defining existence within the transcendental framework of appearing or being-there? I will immediately signal my conclusion: *existence is the name proper to the value of the identity function when this is applied to one and the same element.* It is, so to speak, *the measure of the identity of a thing to itself.*

Given a world and an identity-function taking its values in the transcendental of this world, that which we are going to name the 'existence' of a multiple appearing in this world is the transcendental degree assigned to this multiplicity's self-identity. So defined, existence is a category not of being (mathematics) but of appearing (logic). This entails, in particular, that 'to exist' is meaningless in itself. In keeping with Heidegger's insight – which both Sartre and Merleau-Ponty were to take up – it is only possible to speak of 'existing' in relation to a world. The fact is that existence is a transcendental degree indicating the intensity of a multiplicity's appearing in a given world, and this intensity is in no way prescribed by the pure composition of the multiplicity under consideration.

We can apply to existence the formal remarks made above. If, for example, the degree of identity of a multiple to itself is the maximal degree, this multiple exists in the world without any limitation. In this world, the multiplicity completely affirms its own identity. Symmetrically, if this degree is the minimal degree, this multiple does not exist in this world. The multiple-thing *is* in the world but with an intensity equal to zero. *Its existence is a non-existence.* The thing is in the world but its appearing in the world is the destruction of its identity. Thus, *the being-there of this being is to be an inexistent of the world.*

Often, the existence of a multiplicity in a world is neither maximal nor minimal. The multiplicity exists 'to a certain extent'.

The powerful plane tree of Valéry's poem is given as a complete, unquestionable existence; its existential affirmation knows no limits. It can be said to 'offer itself up' to the world, absolutely identical to itself and all the more affirmative for the fact that its 'candour is bound [. . .] by the force of the site'. In the fleeting world of a car's headlights, on the other hand, the tree – whose merely fugitive presence, quasi-identical to any other, fades like a shadow the very instant it appears – possesses a degree of self-identity, and thus of individual existence, that is weak, though not nil. It is a case of intermediary existence. Finally, while the daydreamer reclining between two trees is vaguely aware of the presence of the other surrounding trees as a blurred haze behind the leaves s/he is so intently gazing at, this presence is, nonetheless, endowed with a minimal self-identity through lack of individuation – there being no shape etched out against the sunlit backdrop by way of which to evaluate it. Any *one* plane tree within this surrounding rippling blur is an inexistent of the world.

The theory of inexistents is highly important since, as we shall see in the next chapter, the fact that there are inexistents renders it necessary for events to occur which drastically change the relation, at a local level, between the multiples of a world and the transcendental legislation of their immanent identities and differences.

At the core of this theory is a veritable

metaphysical theorem. 'Theorem' – because it can be demonstrated using the slightly formalized version of the logic of appearing. 'Metaphysical' – because it consists of a statement that intimately links the appearing of a multiplicity and *the non-appearance of an element of that multiplicity*. 'Metaphysical', also, in that this theorem is conditional upon the fundamental principle of materialism that I mentioned above and depends, therefore, on an orientation in thought that is a philosophical choice and not the result of an argument.

This theorem can be stated very simply as follows: *if a multiplicity appears in a world, one element of this multiplicity, and one alone, is an inexistent of this world*.

It should be noted that the inexistent is not distinguished ontologically; it is not, in any way, that nothing of being-multiple that is the void. 'To inexist' is an existential distinction and, thereby, exclusively internal to appearing. The inexistent is simply that of which the self-identity is measured, in a given world, by the minimal degree.

Let's give an imposing and well-known example. In Marx's analyses of bourgeois or capitalist societies, the proletariat is the inexistent peculiar to

Existence

political multiplicities. It is 'that which does not exist'. This in no way means that it has no being. Marx did not for a second think the proletariat had no being since he was, on the contrary, to pile up volume after volume in the aim of explaining what it is. There is no doubting the social and economic being of the proletariat. Rather, what was doubtful, has always been doubtful and is so today more than ever, is its political *existence*. The proletariat is completely subtracted from the sphere of political presentation. The multiplicity it is can be analysed but, according to the rules governing the appearance of the political world, it does not appear within this. It is there but with the minimal degree of appearance, namely, degree zero. This is obviously what the *Internationale* proclaims: 'We are nothing, let us be all!' What does 'we are nothing' mean? Those proclaiming 'we are nothing' are not in the process of affirming their nothingness. They are simply affirming that they are nothing in the world as it is, as far as appearing politically is involved. From the point of view of their political appearing, they are nothing. Becoming 'all' presupposes, then, a change of world, which is to say, a change of transcendental. The transcendental has to change

61

in order for the assignation to existence and, thus, the inexistent as a multiplicity's point of non-appearing in a world, to change in its turn.

Similarly, until Italian algebraists invented a systematic way of handling 'imaginary' numbers, the square root of a negative real number was assigned a nil degree of self-identity because of its prohibition by the transcendental legislation of the world 'calculation on real numbers'. Such a square root is a conceptual inexistent of this world. Here, again, a mutation in the world of calculation was necessary for it to be possible, once the transcendental regulation of existence had locally changed, to write the symbol 'i' as the mark of existence of the square root of -1.

The demonstration of the existence and unicity of the inexistent for any multiple that accedes to appearing or being-there goes beyond the scope of this book. I would insist on the fact that it depends on the axiom of materialism, namely, that any atom is real. Perhaps one should see in this dependence a dialectical statement: if the world is determined at the level of the One, or atomic level, by a materialist prescription of the type 'appearing = being', then *negation is, in the form of an element struck by inexistence*. This point attests to both the gap between being and existence, and the fact that this gap concentrates, by virtue of the clause of unicity, the power of appearing of the multiple it affects. Which, in turn, clarifies the bond, centred on the inexistent and the scale of which will become evident later on, between a multiple of the world and the power, immanent to this multiple, of the consequences incurred when this is struck by an event.

From this point of view, the doctrine of truths that I am proposing can legitimately claim to adhere to a *materialist dialectic*.

4.1 Philosophy's Existence

If every existence is derived from a transcendental evaluation of a term's self-identity, what about philosophy's existence? And what differentiates this existence twenty years ago (at the time of my first Manifesto) from what can be said of it today (this second Manifesto)?

In 1989, it was still no doubt the case that the transcendental on which philosophy was based remained marked by a general logic of suspicion which set down the norm for all existence in the intellectual world. Let's say that, from the fifties/sixties on, the degree of existence of inherited disciplines – particularly those, including philosophy, proposed by the University at the time – was well nigh declared nil in advance since they were suspected of being nothing but inconsistent validations of the established order. Within the psychoanalytic lineage, Lacan had deciphered philosophical systematization as akin to paranoia.

He described philosophy's discourse as invariably split between the precarious arrogance of
the Master's position and the repetitive weak-
ness of the University. He discredited the 'love
of truth' as an expression devoid of any sense
other than a neurotic one. He accused metaphysics of serving only to 'fill up the hole of politics'.
The modern variants of Marxist revolutionary
politics had, for their part, severely subordinated
philosophy to politics, with Althusser himself of
defining philosophy, brought back to the almost
timeless gestures of the conflict between materialism and idealism, as the 'class struggle in theory'.
The analytical current was to attack philosophy,
as Wittgenstein had already done with brio from
the outset of the twentieth century, as a set of
'meaningless propositions'. It set out to show that
thinking required above all a syntactic supervi-
sion of sentences, on the model of formal logic,
and a semantic surveillance referring to either
the evidence of the senses or the exigencies of
action: empiricism on the one hand, pragmatism
on the other. Finally, in a tortured interpretation
of Nietzsche, Heidegger had declared the end of
metaphysics with the technological completion
of the forgetting of being, and the non-assured

necessity of a return to the origin which, in dialogue with the saying of the poets, would restore the figure of the thinker beyond all philosophy. The post-Second World War, French interpretations of Heidegger compounded this verdict by aligning thinking not only with free existence and revolutionary praxis (Sartre), but also with great poetic or theatrical pronouncements (Beaufret, Char, then Lacoue-Labarthe) and a deconstructive labour within both language and the sensorial spread of experience (Derrida and Nancy).

What is striking about all these configurations is the way in which they end up mobilizing against philosophy the entire range of types of truth: love, desire and drives in the psychoanalytic tradition, politics in the case of the Marxist tradition, science in that of the analytic and art in the Nietzschean. As such, the transcendental, in the name of which philosophy was affirmed to barely exist thirty to forty years ago, may be described as evaluating existences directly on the level of processes of creation, or processes of truth, concluding from philosophy's status as neither a science nor a politics, nor, again, an art or existential passion, that it was condemned to disappear – if it wasn't dead already. Revolution, passionate love, mathematical logic and modern poetry – all multiplicities endowed with an exceptional, practically maximal, intensity of existence in the twentieth century – basically stood between the philosophical tradition and its continuation. Philosophy's self-identity having, as such, become temporally almost nil, it was then possible to mark its inexistence.

My first Manifesto rose up against this verdict by setting truths out as the *conditions* of philosophy, rejecting, under the name of 'suture', any intention to merge philosophy with one of its conditions and making the category of Truth, with its successive elaborations as well as its practical fate, the very core of philosophical labour. Raised up[1] from its inexistence through the transcendental separation of its conditions and returned to an operation of its own, philosophy could go on. To the problematic of its end, I proposed substituting the watchword: 'one more step'. Or that of Beckett's *Unnameable*: 'you must go on'.

We can then describe what is, in a certain sense, the existential necessity of a second Manifesto as follows: if philosophy's existence was declared minimal twenty years ago, one could today maintain that it finds itself no less under threat but for the diametrically opposed reason that it is now endowed with an excessive, artificial existence. Particularly in France, 'philosophy' is everywhere. It serves as a trademark for various media pundits. It livens up cafés and health clubs. It has its magazines and its gurus. It is universally called upon, by everything from banks to major state commissions, to pronounce on ethics, law and duty.

The *raison d'être* of this turnabout is a change of transcendental, relating less to philosophy than to its social substitute, which is ethics. Since the 'new philosophers' and the collapse of socialist states, only the most elementary form of moralizing preaching qualifies any longer as 'philosophy'. All situations are assessed in terms of the moral conduct of their actors, with the number of deaths being the sole yardstick for political endeavours and the fight against the 'bad guys' the unique 'Good' possible to be put forward – in short, what's called 'philosophy' is the sales pitch for what Bush named the fight against the 'Axis of Evil', that hotchpotch of socialist ruins and minuscule fascistic-religious groups in the name of which our West conducts bloody campaigns and defends its indefensible democracy all over the map. It is only possible to exist as a 'philosopher' then, we might say, in so far as one uncritically adopts – in the name of 'democratic' dogma, the refrain of human rights and our societies' various customs in respect of women, types of punishment or the protection of nature – the typically Yankee thesis of the West's moral superiority. This dramatic shift can be formalized as follows: if, twenty years ago, philosophy, forced into ruinous sutures with its conditions of truth, found itself asphyxiated by inexistence, philosophy today, chained to conservative morality, finds itself prostituted by a vacuous over-existence. Whence it is no longer a matter of reaffirming its existence by operations seeking to de-suture it from its conditions, but of setting out its essence *as this is manifested in the world of appearing*, so as to distinguish it from its moral counterfeits. Such counterfeits being, as I have already indicated, all the more virulent for their bolstering the expansion of crass positivism (neurosciences, cognitive science, etc.) by providing its indispensable supplement of soul.

It is a matter today, in sum, of de-moralizing philosophy. This amounts to taking the risk of exposing it once again to the judgement of imposters and sophists – a judgement summed up, as a certain Socrates was to experience, in that gravest of accusations: 'you are corrupting youth'. Only a short while ago, in the pages of a prestigious New York magazine, an American critic published an attack, the complete conceptual mediocrity of which could be allowed to pass given that its aim was exclusively one of moral redress. With regards to young students and misinformed teachers, this prosecutor stated, philosophers such as Slavoj Žižek or myself are nothing less than *reckless*.[2] This is a standard theme intoned by the worst conservatives, from Antiquity right up until today: young people run extremely grave risks if put in contact with 'bad masters' who will divert them from all that is serious and honourable – namely, a career, morality, the family, order, the West, property, law, democracy and capitalism. To avoid such *recklessness*, the first step is to rigorously subordinate conceptual invention to what is obvious or 'natural' in philosophy as these people understand it: namely, a soft morality or what Lacan, in his abrupt way of speaking, termed 'the service of goods'.

As regards the overabundance of existence threatening philosophy today with evaporation into both a conservative and aggressive figure, we will take up a transcendental evaluation of its existence that brings it back towards its essence. By definition, philosophy, when it truly appears, is either *reckless* or it is nothing. As the power of destabilizing dominant opinion, it summons youth to those points where the continuous creation of a new truth is decided. This is the reason why its Manifesto deals today with the typically Platonic movement that conveys forms of appearing to the eternity of truths. This perilous process is one it embarks upon without reservation.

In the world in which we find ourselves, philosophy can only appear as the inexistent peculiar to all morality and all law in so far as morality and law remain, and can but remain, under the heel of the unbelievably inegalitarian violence inflicted upon the world by dominant societies with their savage economy and States that are more than ever – to employ Marx's formula – the mere 'agents of Capital'. Or, put more precisely, philosophy appears in our world when it escapes the status of the inexistent of all morality and all law – when, reversing the verdict that delivers it up to the vacuity of 'philosophies' that are as servile as they are ubiquitous, it acquires the maximal existence of that which illuminates the action of universal truths. This illumination transports philosophy far beyond the figure of 'the human' and its 'rights', far beyond all moralism.

And under these conditions it is, indeed, barely imaginable that a portion of today's youth should recognize a real philosophical upsurge without all that kept them in thrall to the pure and simple perseverance of what is being unremittingly corrupted. Ever eternally is Socrates judged.

5 Mutation

We now know that a truth fully existing in the world can be determined as a maximal degree of self-identity, or will, in any case, be organized around a multiple having this existential property. This condition is, however, a structural one and is, as such, satisfied by all bodies that fully exist in a world. We have yet to identify what makes a truth sufficiently exceptional to the laws of appearing for it to be able to hold universally or from one world to another.

It's impossible to think anything other than that *everything constituting an exception to the laws of the world results from a local modification of these laws themselves*. Or, put more forcefully, albeit not entirely rigorously: every exception to these laws is the result of a law of exception. We must, in other words, assume that a truth is not a body subtracted from the transcendental prescriptions of appearing, but the consequence of a local modification of these prescriptions.

To firmly grasp what this involves, let's define what constitutes a regular or internal change to the laws of appearing. If, for example, a plane tree has a viral disease causing it to lose its leaves and to wither, the system of its relations to the world – for instance, the density of the shadow it casts, greater than that dispensed by the small trees next to it – may well find itself modified. In this case, whereas the degree of identity between its shadow and the shade of its neighbours was previously weak, attesting to the much greater spread of its foliage, this degree now increases and even tends towards the maximal degree as though the great tree found itself reduced to the level of a runt. Not only does this modification not affect the way in which the transcendental is set out but, on the contrary, it presupposes it. It is only with regard to the stability of the relations between degrees and the pertinence of the connection between these degrees and the multiples appearing in the world that we can speak of the tree's decrepitude relative to its recent past. The change remains immanent to the laws. It's a simple *modification*, internal to the logical disposition of the world, a bit like Spinoza's 'mode' is an immanent and necessary inflection of the effects of the only power that exists – that of Substance.

Nor is it possible, moreover, to presuppose a sudden change of the transcendental itself. For the transcendental, strictly speaking, *does not exist*. It is the measure of all existence, without any manifestation being necessary on its part as such. Somewhat similarly, in the case of Spinoza, Substance only exists as the internal production of its effects – the infinite multiplicity of its attributes, in particular – such that it is just as possible to state that Substance alone exists or that only its attributes and modes do. The latter of these alternatives amounts to stating that Substance does not exist. It's the same for the transcendental as the locus of the relations of identity and difference by means of which multiples 'make' world/s. And what does not exist cannot change.

Finally, then, to set about thinking an exception in what appears (or in what occurs, for it is the same thing – being, for its part, *does not occur*, it simply is), we need to locate this in *the relation between a multiplicity and the transcendental. A* multiplicity – because whatever occurs is always local; the idea of a global exception makes no sense, for what would this be an exception to, given that everything is changed? Its *relation* with the transcendental – because this is what arrays the possibilities of appearing as such. Yet the relation between a determined multiplicity and the transcendental is precisely this multiplicity's appearing, evaluating the immanent relations of identities and differences between all its elements. We do not see how this relation as such can change in its principle without the world changing.

It is, therefore, absolutely necessary to admit that real change, or mutation, consists in neither a global change of the transcendental nor a change of the mode by which a multiple's elements are differentially evaluated by transcendental degrees. The only possibility is that a multiple is introduced in some sort of supplementary way within the register of appearing.

Yet how can a multiple that is *already there* in the world and, therefore, already evaluated as regards its immanent resources in the register of appearing, *supplement* the operation of transcendental rules? Or must we, rather, envisage a multiple's emanating from outside the world, like a meteorite of appearing? But why this one rather than another? All this seems the order of miracles. We must, much rather, rationally assume:

(i)   that the multiple localizing the mutation is well and truly already there in the world, that it appears there;

(ii)   that the transcendental of the world concerned is not modified in its internal rules;

(iii) that the supplementation by the multiple concerned maintains some relation with its link to the transcendental, for this supplementation would otherwise be floating or rootless with respect to this multiple's appearing as assumed in condition (i) above.

The only option left open to us is to pose *that there is a local mutation in appearing when a multiple itself falls under the measurement of identities rendering the comparison of its elements possible. Or, put another way, when appearing's basis in being comes to appear locally.*

Normally, a multiple is inscribed in the world by a degree of identity being assigned to every pair of its elements (see *Schema 1* inside the cover flap). A fundamental ontological law (commented on in *Being and Event*, Meditation 18) prohibits, however, any multiple from being an element of itself. As a result, the transcendental evaluation of identities and differences for any given multiple is immanent to this multiple, without the latter *itself* being taken into consideration. The measurement of the degrees of identity between the elements of the plane tree (such and such a leaf, or a branch and a root, etc.) operates element by element but does not include the plane tree itself. There is not, *internally to the inscription of the plane tree within the world*, any determination of a degree of identity between, say, the plane tree and a piece of its bark. Such a degree of identity can, of course, be part of a multiple's appearing in the world but *this multiple will not be the plane tree*, any more than it will be the piece of bark: it has to contain both one and the other as elements.

If, then, it so happens that a multiple falls under the protocol that immanently evaluates the network of relations constituting its appearing, there is an obvious transgression of the ontological and logical complex that brings a multiple-being into appearing. This transgression however, no more presupposes a supplementary multiple or a modification of the transcendental than it does an arbitrary indifference of the multiple's relation to its new 'entry' within appearing because *it is under its own law of appearance that the multiple comes to be counted.* As such, we satisfy the three conditions deduced above.

We will name 'site' a multiple that comes to appear in a new way in so far as it falls under the general measurement of the degrees of identity prescribing, element by element, its own appearing. Let's say that *a site itself is made to appear (of itself).*[1]

Such is the formal principle of a mutation in appearing. A concise analysis shows there to be three types of mutation. First of all, according to the degree of existence possessed by the multiple when it falls under its own transcendental connection, the mutation is said to be a *fact* if this degree is not maximal. Implying a local anomaly in the distribution of appearing's relations, facts are more than the regular changes or modifications 'à la Spinoza' we spoke of above but, nevertheless, remain largely internal to appearing in its general form. Then, those sites having a maximal existential value are distinguished on the basis of the consequences, and hence the power, of the local mutation. In chapter 4 we saw that every multiple possesses one, and only one, inexistent element. If this inexistent element remains invariable or simply acquires, under the effect of the mutation, an existence less than the maximum, the mutation will be described as a *weak singularity*. If the inexistent acquires a maximal existential value, the multiple will be said to be an *event*.

In other words, an event is a site (a multiple itself falling under the law making its elements appear) that is in excess of both facts (for the site's value of existence is maximal) and weak singularities (for the inexistent, for its part, equally comes to exist with the maximal value).

It is to be carefully noted that the characteristics of the event consist of: reflexivity (the site belongs to itself, at least fleetingly, such that its multiple-being comes to the surface of its appearing 'in person'); intensity (it exists maximally); and power (its effect extends as far as a complete raising up of the inexistent, from the minimal or nil value to the maximal value: 'We are nothing, let us be all', as sung in the *Internationale*).

Of course, when it comes to giving an example of an event, we are unable to confine ourselves to empirical plane trees. I've proposed a great number of detailed examples in *Logics of Worlds*, of which we can cite here: the insurrection of slaves under Spartacus' leadership or the first day of the Paris Commune, in politics; the Chauvet cave artists' paintings of horses or the architecture of Brasilia, in the arts; Julie and Saint-Preux in Rousseau's novel *The New Heloise* or Dido and Aeneas in Berlioz's opera *The Trojans*, in love; and Galois' invention of the theory of groups or Euclid's presentation of the theory of prime numbers, in science. What appears implicitly in all of these is the decisive thesis of this entire little book: namely, *a truth can only originate in an event*.

That a truth is universal makes it necessary to maintain that its process binds universality to pure contingency – that of the event. A truth appears in the world as the surnumerary connection of chance and eternity.

This is why we can return to the plane tree in its poetic form, for surely such a connection is what Valéry has in mind when the plane tree responds furiously to the attempt to reduce it to its particular appearance or, again, when it sets against this particularity its own inclusion within the universal. Let us read its response, hearing in 'tempest' the action of the event and in its 'superb head' the plane tree's incorporation within the universal consequences of the tempest or a truth's advent in the world. This 'superb head' is the glorious body of the transfigured tree, which is also, thereby, the generic equal of all that grows, with tree and grass joined, under the fold of the True, in fraternity:

> No! says the tree. It says *No!* by its superb
>   head's
> Scintillating sparks,
> Treated universally by the tempest
> As it does a blade of grass.[2]

6 Incorporation

Let an event have taken place – it will, as such, have vanished, for the transcendental pathology constituted by the coming to appearance's surface of its basis in being (a multiple, subjected to the evaluation of its elements in terms of their identity) is incapable of setting in or of lasting. All that remains are its consequences, among which is that defining the evental value of the site: namely, the raising up of its inexistent element, which passes from the minimal or nil degree to the maximal one.

Every truth is dependent upon something whose existence had been totally unapparent acceding to the flush of appearance: in politics, ancient slaves or contemporary proletariats; in art, that which had been without any formal value suddenly finding itself transfigured by an unforeseeable shift of the boundary demarcating what is recognized as form, even when de-formed, from what is relegated to formlessness; in love, every fracturing of the solidity of the One by an improbable and long-denied Two that experiments with the world on its own account and dedicates itself to the infinity of this experimentation; in science, the submission to the letter of mathematics of a whole span of material or vital qualities that had seemed to be its contrary. With the proper names linked to these upsurges being: Spartacus or Lenin, Aeschylus or Nicolas de Staël, Heloise and Abelard, just like Edith Piaf and Marcel Cerdan, Archimedes or Galileo.

We are going to name the inexistent of a previous state of the world that finds itself raised up or elevated to the maximal power of appearing by the evental mutation: a *primordial statement*. This is not because it's necessarily a matter of something said, but because the term in question is equivalent to a sort of commandment. It says to us, from the heights of the authority granted it by its having been raised up: 'See what is coming to pass and not only what is. Work for the consequences of the new. Accept the discipline appropriate to these consequences' becoming. Make of the whole multiple you are, bodies within a body, the ineffaceable matter of the True.' These material imperatives declare to us things such as: 'Workers of the world, unite!' (Marx); 'The world is written in the language of mathematics' (Galileo); 'A throw of the dice will never abolish chance' (Mallarmé); or 'Love is a thought' (Pessoa).

Initiated by the primordial statement, a new body forms in the world that will be the body of truth or subjectivizable body and which we will often, when the context is clear, simply call *body*. How is this body formed? This depends on the affinities between the other bodies of the world and the primordial statement. The latter is the rallying point for the multiples that become involved in the process of unfurling the consequences of the event – with these consequences having both their concentrated source and the justification of their novelty in this statement. Think of the 'leftists' forming, up until roughly the end of the seventies, the innumerable and heterogeneous group of those faithful to May 68. Think of the lovers brought into the world by the transporting effects of that 'I love you' that affixes in a primordial statement the fleetingness of an encounter. Picture the artistic and worldly asceticism of the great students and disciples of Schoenberg,

Berg and Webern after the dodecaphonic turn of the first decade of the twentieth century. Or, again, note the bedazzlement with which French mathematicians in the 1930s were to discover the radical innovation of modern algebra borne by the inventions of the German school, Emmy Noether first of all. Thousands of other examples show what it entails, for an individual rallied by the authority of a primordial statement, to declare him- or herself, body and soul, on the side of this statement and a confirmed volunteer for the incorporated (and reiterated: 'encore!') unfurling of its effects.[1]

For this process consists of the adjunction, to a body in the making, of everything that tests out an essential affinity with what this body unfurls by way of the consequences of the statement and, hence, of the event that, like a bolt of lightning, was to strike the laws of appearing at a precise point. This is why the appropriate name for this process is: *incorporation*.

Incorporation can be formalized by using the most intricate details of the logic of appearing. This task is carried out in *Logics of Worlds*, particularly in Book VII, which contains the theory of the body of truth, but it presupposes all the refinements of the 'Great Logic', explained notably in Book III. Here we are simply going to describe what is at stake.

What is meant by an 'affinity' between some body or other and the primordial statement that is the trace of an event in a world? The rudiments of the theory of appearing set out in chapters 3 and 4 of this book are all we need to understand this. The statement – the raising up of an inexistent – is from then on a multiple that appears in the world with a maximal value. Thus, the primordial statement of a love, that 'I love you' of the aptly named 'declarations of love', exists in the sub-jective world of lovers, or future lovers, with an intensity that nothing else can surpass. Consider, as a result, any multiple whatsoever of the world concerned – for example, the pleasure one of the lovers takes in walks along the beach. This element will be said to incorporate itself within the body of amorous truth in the process of constituting itself if its relation of identity to the primordial statement is measured by the highest possible degree. In practical terms, what this means, of course, is that the lover in question wants to get the other to come along on walks of this kind, to include them in his or her passion for deserted beaches, to re-evaluate his or her love of the sea's murmuring from the standpoint of love and nothing else, and so on. Put formally, this means that the degree of identity between the datum 'pleasure in walks along the beach' and the primordial statement of love cannot be less than the degree of existence accruing to this pleasure. The meaning, therefore, is clear: henceforth, a personal affect can only enter into the composition of the body of love if its identity to the amorous primordial statement is not smaller than its own intensity or if it can be 'composed' with the love without losing any of its force. It then enriches the body of love, which is to say that it enters into the process of a truth: the seashore, as a fragment of appearing, is re-evaluated from the point of the Two and is no longer immured in narcissistic enjoyment of the world.[2]

This empirical picture is reinforced by formal analysis, which, indeed, demonstrates that if a multiple of the world appears with a maximal intensity of existence (as is the case, by definition, for every primordial statement), the relation of identity that any multiple whatsoever appearing in the same world has with this first multiple cannot be of a greater degree than that of the existence of the second multiple: the degree of identity of any multiple with a primordial statement is at most equal to the degree of existence of the multiple concerned. If it is equal, then it is as high as it can be: its relation of identity with the primordial statement is maximal. This is what is denoted by its profound 'affinity' with the statement.

We will, then, say that *a multiple of the world is incorporated within a truth process, or becomes a component of the body of this truth, if its degree of identity to the primordial statement is maximal.* Such is the case of the young leftist who is carried beyond herself by her adhesion without limits to the effects of the event 'May 68', the primordial statement of which might be said to be 'Let's reinvent politics'. So too is it the case of the pleasure the lover takes in walks along the beach when these strolls become, under the injunction of 'I love you', ecstatic moments of the love itself.

Incorporating yourself within a truth's becoming consists in bringing to the body serving as the support of this truth everything within you that has an intensity comparable to what it is that allows you to identify with the primordial statement – qua the stigmata of the event in which the body has its source.

Unable to enter into details here, I would but finally note that: a truth process is the construction of a new body that appears gradually in the world as all the multiples having an authentic affinity with a primordial statement are drawn together around the latter. And as the primordial statement is the trace of an event's power, we can also say that a body of truth results from the incorporation within the consequences of an event of everything, within the world, that has been maximally impacted by its power.

A truth is, then, an event having vanished whose unforeseeable body the world causes to appear little by little in appearing's disparate materials.

7 Subjectivation

We are now assuming the existence of a body of truth as constituted around a primordial statement, itself the trace of a vanished event. This body is situated in the world affected by the event and visibly evolves there. Thus, *the position taken up in relation to the existence of this body is the real*, with this being the *materiality of the position taken up in relation to the event*. But an event is a perturbation of the world's order (since it locally disrupts the logical organization – the transcendental – of this world), as the raising up of the inexistent attests. The position taken up in relation to the new body amounts, then, to a position with respect to the order of the world and to what must or must not exist in this world.

Abstractly, it is clear that we are going to have three types of positions. We've described the first in the previous chapter: incorporation within the body, enthusiasm for what is new, and active fidelity to that having locally disrupted the laws of the world through its advent. The second is indifference: to act as though nothing has taken place or, more exactly, to be convinced that, were the event not to have occurred, things would be basically the same. This is the classic reactive position, which quashes what is new within the soft power of conservation. The third is hostility: to consider the new body as a malevolent foreign irruption that must be destroyed. In this hatred of the new, of all that is 'modern' and different from tradition, we recognize obscurantism.

We will call these attitudes the body's *subjectivations* and set down three types of subjectivation that prescribe, relative to the subjectivizable body, three types of subject: faithful, reactive and obscure.

What must be firmly grasped is that the three subjects are contemporaneous with the event and the body, even if this contemporaneity is negative. They are, as a result, new figures. The reactive subject must be acknowledged to be an invention of conservatism, however paradoxical this sounds, and the obscure subject to be, itself, a creation internal to the most obtuse of traditions. In so far as they define *orientations in respect of the body*, these three subjective types partake of that which is new. All three are figures of the active present in which a hitherto unknown truth plots its course. They make up a history in which a truth wends its way with difficulty, wresting itself, through its universality, from the circumstances of its appearance.

Take, for example, that typical instance of an event's upsurge that is the October 17 Revolution in Russia. The new body is obviously constituted by both the Soviet State (which is, in fact, the becoming-State of the Party) and the Communist Parties that are created all over the world from 1920 on and form the Third International.

The faithful subject is the incorporation – which is to say, system – of individual adhesions to this complex of national States, parties and international organization defining the worldwide Communist movement. As the militant orientation of its becoming, *the faithful subject plots the present of the body as the new time of a truth*.

The reactive subject is everything that orientates the conservation of previous economic and political forms (capitalism and parliamentary democracy) under the conditions of existence of the new body. It is the bourgeois democratic subject ensuring its perenniality. In one sense, the reactive subject denies the event's effectiveness since it maintains that the previous world can and should go on as it is. It preserves an insurmountable distance between itself and the new political present. It transforms its non-presence to the new present into a false present. Yet, in another sense, it accords the utmost consideration to the new body's existence. In particular, under various forms (the labour movement in England, the reforms brought in by the Popular Front and the Liberation in France, the New Deal in the United States . . .), it will multiply the concessions made to workers, drawing up a social policy and curbing the unlimited appetites of financial and industrial powers, on condition that all this remains within the framework of the previous order (identities and differences being evaluated under the law of the same transcendental). These 'reforms' are obviously required to make sure that the incorporation within the process of truth, the expansion of the faithful subject and the active Communist conviction stay within appropriate limits. Overall, the appearing of the previous world has to remain under the same transcendental, such that the new body is only able to deploy its maximal existence locally. This is what the orientation assigned to this body by the reactive subject comes down to: that it should stay put in its corner as far as possible. The American State has defined this line, with respect to the Communist universe, as a line of *containment*.[1] In this sense, the reactive subject is a new subject induced by the new body: it assures the *invention of new conservative practices*. By creating new ways of keeping the present of the True at a distance, it maintains the semblance of continuity. It is the present of the dissimulation of the present.

The obscure subject wants the death of the new body. The perenniality of the transcendental at the price of immanent reforms is not enough for it. This is what defined the fascist line in the first half of the twentieth century in Europe. What makes this line revolutionary is that, in order to have done with the presence of the new present, it is necessary to render present the integral destruction of the body of truth, which means liquidating the faithful subject in all its forms since the faithful subject is the orientation of this body. The problem of the obscure subject is that this purely counter-revolutionary dimension of its revolution lacks sufficient power to rally the destructive forces it needs. It must, additionally, come up with a completely fictitious body that rivals the body of truth even while, however, rejecting and denying, rather than ratifying, the event in which its rival originates. For this, *the body that fascism claims to represent has to be of the order not of an event but of a substance*: a Race, a Culture, a Nation or a God. Accordingly, the obscure subject will, first, impose the lethal sovereignty of a fictitious body borrowed from the tradition and, then, destroy the new present by a paradoxical present which is that of eternal substance. The obscure subject makes a present of that which, by its account, has always been there but which events have deformed and dissimulated. This is the real meaning of the 'thousand year Reich' promised by Hitler: once the present of revolutions – especially the Communist present – was destroyed, the present of Aryan or German eternity would prevail. To the mobile body of the truth process, the obscure subject opposes the fixed past-present of national, racial or religious substance. But this promise is untenable. Unlike the body of truth, unfurling that which results from the real of the event, the body of the obscure subject is fictitious and, as such, only derives its apparent present from the destruction of its rival. Aryan eternity only existed as long as did the extermination of the Jews (which explains why the Nazis applied themselves to this right up to the last second of their existence). The Reich existed only as long as it took to lose the war (which explains the suicidal refusal of any negotiation, even after the invasion of Germany). The obscure subject derives all its present from the fierce resistance of the body of truth. It is the making-present, under the blazon of death, of the faithful subject's tenacity.

The shifting configuration of these three subjective types defines a (political, artistic, scientific or amorous) historical sequence. One sees, for example, the reactive subject ally itself with the obscure subject against the faithful subject (in Germany, the classic reactionary forces' handing over to Hitler the lead against the Communists), the faithful subject ally itself with the reactive subject against the obscure subject (the alliance of the US and the USSR against the Nazis), and even the temptation – in truth, always suicidal – of an alliance between the faithful and obscure subjects[2] (the 1939 Germano-Soviet pact). This is because *the historical present, contrary to what the Hegelian dialectic and dogmatic Marxism affirm, does not coincide with the body of truth's present.* Indeed, History is always the imbrication of the three subjective types, combining, as regards the body-of-truth, this body's three orientations. Merleau-Ponty, noting the apparent dissimulation of a truth's becoming in its present itself, was to declare that 'History never confesses'.[3] The truth is that it is only incomprehensible for whosoever refuses to decipher the stigmata of the present. It is necessary to first attend, patiently, to events and the ensuing constructions of truths. Then to accept that reaction and its extreme forms are also innovations, contemporaneous with the post-evental present signalled by the subjectiviz-able body. And, finally, to hold that the confused appearance of History is due to the impossibility of calculating what the result of the subjective orientations' mixture will be. For the True can only be known to the extent that, in the course of the various episodes pitting it against reactive or obscure innovations, it will have attained the eternity of which it is capable. As a result, it will only be known – which is what is called 'knowing' – as detached from its present and, hence, from the confused world having witnessed its birth. Only when it is set out in another world, in order to be used for the purposes of new incorporations, will its resurrection deliver it up to us as such. A truth is only universal in the future perfect of the corporeal process that caused it to appear.

One shouldn't assume that politics, and it alone, is paradigmatic as concerns truths' evental becoming and the subject-forms accompanying this. I would like to show this here by speaking of love.

We have seen that the body of love is a particular form of experimenting with the world enacted from the point of view of the Two. The individuals summoned to the incorporation are two to act as the bearers of this Two, such that they constitute a minimal 'collectivity'. This in no way prevents the history of a love being just as confused an entanglement as the history of an emancipatory politics (or true politics), the history of a new regime of art or the implementation of a new scientific theory.

The subjective types are, in particular, easily recognizable.

Naturally, the faithful subject is everything that orientates love towards the effective power of the Two it institutes. It is the incorporation itself, the fact that ever more fragments of the world, of an ever greater intensity, appear before the Two instead of being folded up within narcissistic satisfaction or dissatisfaction. Let us note in passing that love is like an atom of universality – not transcultural universality (political internationalism, the scientific community, and so on) but transindividual universality. Passing from one to two, and experimenting with the Two to infinity (since every element of the world is capable of being treated by a body of love), love is the first degree of the individual's passage to an immediate beyond her- or himself. It is the elementary form of singularity's sublimation in universality. This is why, as we know, humanity has, since time immemorial, been fascinated by love and love stories. What is spelt out within love is that living – what is called living – comes down, not to individual interests, but to the manner in which the world is exposed to 'us', however limited this 'us' may be and however hazardous may prove its uncertain construction not from what is but from what befalls 'us'.

The reactive subject in love precisely refuses to assume this risk without solid guarantees. It demands, in a certain sense, that the lover can say life goes on just as it was, with love being, as a result, not a radical event but a sort of inner complement necessary for a satisfying existence. To this end, the body of love is filtered by all sorts of conservative precautions taking the general form of a contract: I need to know whether I derive more advantages than disadvantages from life in a couple and also whether my individual advantages are equivalent to those my partner derives from the situation. We can name 'conjugality' this juridically cautious vision attempting to circumscribe as narrowly as possible the undomesticated and unequal share presupposed by love's very origin: an incalculable encounter that destines life to the blind experimentation of its consequences. Little by little, the reactive subject metamorphoses love into that which is both its objective substratum and its permanent enemy: the family. This subject is what guarantees that love can and must assure the transition from one family to another. Now, the family occupies exactly the same position in relation to love as the State does in relation to politics. In this sense, reactive conjugality is strictly equivalent to the 'democracy' that today one is trying to impose upon the whole world – including by the use of arms. As we know, this 'democracy' is politics without politics, since its one and only purpose is to make sure that capitalist-parliamentarianism, that is, the dominant form of the modern State, perseveres without serious upheavals. In this sense, conjugality is love without love. It seeks to make sure that the nuclear family perseveres.

The obscure subject, in love, takes up a revolutionary position just as it does in politics. In no way is it satisfied with conjugality. It proclaims that, far from being the product of chance, love is already written in the stars or, in any case, in a necessity overwhelmingly vaster than its apparent contingency. It is set on tracking down and destroying every trace of this contingency in which it sees only a lethal risk – that of the other's leaving or being unfaithful. To combat love's being without any sort of guarantee, other than its very process, it has to propose a fiction to it as well, with this fiction being that of the One: for the obscure subject, love in no way entails the infinity of the world coming before the Two that an event has rendered topical; it is the fusional assumption of the predestined One. In this deadly vision (as shown by the Wagnerian myth of Tristan and

Isolde) the most common operator of destruction is jealousy. The jealous lover, indeed, leaves love no share of freedom or peregrination. Any deviation in respect of the supposed One is the point of departure of a betrayal. Everything that evokes contingency is an injury inflicted upon the supposed One. Everything that does not repeat the fusional pact, everything that affirms the Two, is suspect. Jealousy is the experimentation of this suspicion and the subjective spur of amorous obscurantism. Just like fascism in what concerns the life of a society, jealousy transforms the life of a couple into an ongoing saga of policing. And just like fascism, it prefers annihilation to the breakdown of the One.

Those, like Proust, who think that jealousy is the essence of love are similar to nationalist extremists who think that the essence of the community is the archetypal One of its empirical or racial existence. The only way they can sustain their vision in the long run is by torture, both of themselves and others, and finally by murder, whether real or symbolic.

But all real love struggles, as does true politics, to save the faithful subject – who leaves open the risk of the Two – from being excessively eaten

away at or undone by the actions, always contemporaneous with the body it orientates, of the
reactive and obscure subjects. Between the indis-
tinct family and deadly jealousy, love must take
up the wager of its moving eternity.

8 Ideation

I name 'Idea' that upon which an individual's representation of the world, including her- or himself, is based once s/he is bound to the faithful subject type through incorporation within the process of a truth. The Idea is that which makes the life of an individual, a human animal, orientate itself according to the True. Or, put another way: the Idea is the mediation between the individual and the Subject of a truth – with 'Subject' designating here that which orientates a post-evental body in the world.

This sense of the word 'Idea' instantiates my own interpretation of the Platonic idea, and particularly the 'idea of the Good' to which a passage, as famous as it is enigmatic, is devoted in the *Republic*. By replacing the word 'Good' – used by too many moralizing theologies from the early Neoplatonists on – with that of 'True', we can obtain the following translation of Plato's words:

Only inasmuch as it is in truth can that which is knowable be said to be known in its being. Yet, to the Idea of the True, or Truth, it owes not only its being known in its being, but also its known-being itself, namely, that which, of its being, can only be said 'being' inasmuch as it is exposed to thought. Truth itself, however, is not of the order of that which is exposed to thought, for it is the raising up of this order and therefore finds itself imparted a distinct function, both in terms of precedence and of power.[1]

Plato's problem – which is still ours – is how our experience of a particular world (that which we are given to know, the 'knowable') can open up access to eternal, universal and, in this sense, transmundane truths. For this to come about, according to Plato, this experience must be set out 'in truth', with this immanence being under-stood in the strict sense that only inasmuch as it is set out *in* the element of truth can a particular object of the world of our experience be said to be known, not only in its particularity but in its very being. That this object of the world is then grasped in its being, he adds, is because there is situated 'in' truth that share of the object which only is in so far as it is exposed to thought. We are, as a result, at the point where the being of the object is indiscernible from what, of this being, is thinkable. This point of indiscernibility between the particularity of the object and the universality of the thought of the object is exactly what Plato names the Idea. Finally, as for the Idea itself, given that it only exists in its power to bring forth the object 'in truth' and, hence, to uphold that there is something universal, it is not itself presentable because it *is* the presentation-to-the-true. In a word: there is no Idea of the Idea. This absence, moreover, can be named 'Truth'. Exposing the thing in truth, the Idea is true and is, therefore, always the idea of the True, but the True is not an idea.

The configuration I'm proposing, by way of philosophy's salvation, is basically a materialist transposition of this Platonic vision – unless, that is, Plato himself were already a materialist and to have created a *materialism of the Idea*. First, the individual supports of a possible thought that we human animals capable of eternity are, exist in the appearance of worlds that do not expose anything true by themselves. Worlds are only the matter of their transcendental logic, and we

are examples amongst others of the play of differences and identities between multiples ruled
by these logics. Second, it sometimes happens
(event, or, for Plato, 'conversion') that we are able
to enter into the setting-out of a truth. Admittedly,
this process for us is neither an ascension nor
linked to the death of a body and the immortality of a soul. It is, as Plato also knew, a dialectic
– that of the incorporation of our individual life
within the new body constituted around the primordial statement, that trace of the event. In this
way, we pass from the figure of the individual to
that of the Subject, just as with the Greek master
we pass from sophistry (the cunning, and truth-
less, accommodation to the differential laws of
the world) to philosophy – except that, in the
place of philosophy, we have art, science, politics
or love; philosophy being for us but a secondary
capture of these in the light of a concept of Truth.

Entering into the composition of a Subject orientates our individual existence while, for Plato,
dialectical conversion renders possible a just life.
This 'entry into truth' is what the Idea brings about.
If we replace ascending metaphors (one 'rises'
towards the Idea from the world as perceived
by the senses) by horizontal ones (the individual

108

lives incorporated within the process of a body of truth's development are orientated in the world by this process in accordance with a heteronomous law, producing thereby a universal truth the material of which is, nevertheless, completely particular), it is clear that the Idea is nothing other than that by which individuals discover within themselves the action of thought as immanence to the True. This discovery immediately indicates both that the individual is not the author of this thought but merely that through which it passes, and that this thought would, nevertheless, not have existed without all the incorporations which make up its materiality. Just as Plato is able to declare that the just life is achieved only by the dialectical opening-up to Ideas, so too I would declare that it is in so far as living individuals enter into truth and, hence, into the composition of a subjectivizable body that they experiment with the universal. For they know both that what they participate within is valid for everyone, with their participation thereby affording them no particular right, and that their life is, however, raised up and accomplished by having participated in this way in something beyond their simple subsistence. This knowledge is that of the Idea.

Let's say that a true life is the result of an *Ideation*.

Deleuze forcefully maintained – against, it must be said, all the joyous, 'anarcho-desiring' and spontaneist interpretations of his philosophy – that thinking is never a matter of voluntary decision or natural inclination. We are always, he declared, *forced* to think. Thought pushes us, as it were, from behind. It is neither lovable nor desired. Thought is a violence done unto us. I utterly agree with this view. It seems to me, moreover, to be altogether a Platonic one. Who is not aware of the violence – certainly charming and subtle but no less implacable – that Socrates brings to bear upon his interlocutors? In what I'm proposing there is a double constraint. First, there is the brutal contingency of the event that exposes us to a choice that we have not desired: incorporation, indifference, or hostility?; the faithful subject, the reactive subject, or the obscure subject? Then, there is the construction, point by point, of the body which subjects individuals to previously unknown forms of discipline, whether it be a matter of new forms of mathematical demonstration, amorous fidelity and Party cohesion, or of giving up the delectation of long-established

110

artistic forms for the sacrificial asperity of the avant-gardes. This, too, is Ideation: the representation of the universal power of something whose immediate particularity is very often perilous, unstable and a source of anguish by dint of being guaranteed by nothing at all.

I would like to make this theory of the Idea as the exposing of the mere individual to her/his becoming-Subject as concrete as possible. Let's take, for example, the case of Cantor, the late nineteenth-century inventor of mathematical set theory. The event in which his work originates is the history of Analysis and its wrestling with the notion of the infinite. At the start of the century, Cauchy's work had consisted in ridding differential and integral calculus of any reference to the 'infinitely small', which had, throughout the eighteenth century, both constituted its underlying metaphysics and already been severely criticized by philosophers, Berkeley in particular. A quantity a was said to be 'infinitely close' to a quantity b if the difference $a - b$ was an 'infinitely small' quantity. But what was meant by an infinitely small quantity? No one knew. Cauchy replaced all this by the dynamic notion of a series' limit, thereby furnishing Analysis with reliable axiomatic foundations and jettisoning from mathematical thought any idea of the actual infinite. With Bolzano and Dedekind, however, the ontology of all this was understood to be too weak and, above all, largely physical or empiricist. When you say that a series 'tends towards' a limit, the underlying schema is that of movement, with mathematics being, in fact, under the yoke of intuitions relating to the representation of space. To return to purely mathematical schemas, it was necessary to retackle the concept of the actual infinite and to assume that infinite quantities exist. But how can this be done if our idea of the infinite remains terribly vague, as was the case with the 'infinitely small'? Cantor resolved this problem by creating the generic concept of *set* and by making new 'numbers' – the ordinals and the cardinals – correspond, through strictly rational procedures, to infinite sets. This most certainly constitutes one of the most admirable universal creations in the whole of human history. It is clear that the body of truth here is what achieves, in the world of calculus, a new appropriation of the predicate 'infinite' for numbers from which this predicate was rationally separated (any number, taken rigorously,

measured by definition a finite quantity).[2] As
to how Cantor achieved his own incorporation
within the process of this new truth, this was
through an extraordinarily tormented Ideation.
Indeed, he fully grasped that the thought passing
through him, and which he was one of the first
to organize, equally radically changed mathematical rationality's relations to philosophy and to
religion. Until his breakthrough, the Infinite had
been linked to the One in the conceptual form of
the God of religions or metaphysical systems. The
domain of human thought was the finite, with our
being essentially creatures doomed to finitude.
This is the very reason why, moreover, Cauchy
strictly kept the notion of limit away from any
form of compromise with an actual infinite. With
Cantor, the infinite was to enter into the domain
of the multiple. Not only did he assume the actual
existence of infinite multiplicities but he demonstrated that there exists an infinity of different
infinites. That being the case, how, then, was one
to deal with the relation between human animals'
thought (the individual Cantor as incorporated
within the deployment of the rational theory
of infinite numbers) and the supposition of a
Transcendence (the individual Cantor as a faithful

113

Christian) if the opposition of the finite and infinite, or the multiple and the One, no longer suffices? Cantorian Ideation deals wholly with this point and is, as a result, the exposure to thought of the radical, transgressive and universal innovation of its own invention. From then on, Cantor was to seek a way of introducing the difference between the mathematical infinite and the theological infinite within the very concept of the infinite, without being greatly convinced himself. He was to write to the Roman Curia to seek counsel. He was also to go mad . . . Here, then, we can understand the way in which Ideation organized his heroic determination and his demonstrative discipline right up to the limits of the unintelligible: after having given a rigorous proof of the fact that the set of rational numbers – the fractions – is denumerable and, hence, that these numbers, contrary to our entire immediate intuition, are not 'more numerous' than natural whole numbers, he was to exclaim: 'I see it but I don't believe it!' However, we also understand the way in which, on the other hand, Ideation organized and modified the relation of the individual Cantor to the ordinary world, expressing his quality of an animal of this world who, tormented and almost

114

shattered by the ontological violence of his think-ing incorporation, was nevertheless not to give in.

Schema 2 (found inside the back cover flap) presents truths' complete trajectory and is, there-fore, a sort of condensation of the whole of *Logics of Worlds*. There is no question of our comment-ing on it here in detail. We will simply signal that the line which goes from 'indifferent multiplici-ties' to the eventental rupture organizes the *objec-tive* supports of a truth's construction, which are really given in a world, whereas the line which goes from the event to 'eternal truths' sets out the *subjective* categories induced by individuals' incorporation within the becoming of this truth. Between these two lines, there is a vertical corre-spondence. For example, as we have explained, the subjective trace of an event is nothing other than the raising up of an inexistent. Likewise, the condition of an existence belongs to the transcen-dental. Or, again, the organs of a body of truth serve to deal with the points of the world under the form of a radical choice, and so on.

If one admits that Ideation is that which, in the individual undergoing incorporation within the process of a truth, is responsible for binding together the components of this trajectory, then one understands that it is that through which a human life is universalized – at the cost, clearly, of difficult problems with its particularity.

The Idea is the severity of the sense of existence.

Conclusion

Comparing this second Manifesto to the first, as I've already undertaken to do on the question of philosophy's existence in chapter 4.I, I am struck by five points, which constitute just as many symptomatic traits of the way in which the world has changed these last twenty years.

1. As I've already stated, the philosophical position I combated twenty years ago was principally the Heideggerian position in its French variants (Derrida, Lacoue-Labarthe, Nancy, but also Lyotard), which consisted in announcing the irremediable end of philosophy in its metaphysical form and considering the arts, poetry, painting and theatre as proffering the supreme recourse for thought. My 'Platonic gesture' was to reaffirm the possibility of philosophy in its original sense – namely, the articulation (transformed, of course, but no less recognizable) of a crucial categorical triplet: that of being, the subject and

117

truth. I maintained that philosophy had to subtract itself from the pathos of the end, that it was
not in a particularly new, dramatic moment of
its history, and that it needed, then as always, to
attempt to go a step further with its constituent
propositions – principally by the construction of a
new concept of truth or truths. I set myself up, in
sum, against the critical ideal of deconstruction.

Today, the main adversaries are no longer
the same. On one of the last occasions I met
with Derrida – for we had made peace with one
another – he said to me: 'In any case, today we
have the same enemies'. This was exactly right.
The target of this second Manifesto is no longer
the surpassing of Metaphysics under the guise of
its deconstruction. Much rather, it is directed at the
reconstitution – as happens whenever intellectual
reaction, buoyed by the success of reactive forces
per se, gains momentum – of something like a
poor dogmatism by way of analytical philosophy,
cognitive science and the ideology of democracy
and human rights. Namely, a sort of scientism
stipulating the mind must be naturalized and
studied according to the experimental protocols
of neurology, reinforced, as always, by an inane
moralism with a religious tinge – in substance:

one has to be nice and democratic rather than nasty and totalitarian. This is why, when I constantly stress the triplet of being, the subject and truth, what's at issue is its *effective* appearance or observable action in the world since this is what scientism (which knows only the naturalness of objects, never the immortality of subjects) and moralism (which knows only the subject of law and order, never that of radical choice and creative violence) seek to deny exists. Let's say that a Manifesto for philosophy's continued *existence* (against the pathos of its accomplishment) has been succeeded by a Manifesto dedicated to its revolutionary *pertinence* (against the servile dogmatism making it a component of Western propaganda).

2. In the first Manifesto, I declared for the first time that philosophy's existence depends on four types of generic conditions or truth procedures: emancipatory politics and its variants, formal and experimental sciences (mathematics and physics), the arts (the plastic arts, music, poetry and literature, theatre, dance and cinema) and love. I set out the modernity of some of these conditions: Leninism and Maoism, the Cantorian revolution, the age of poets from its opening by Hölderlin

until its closure by Paul Celan, psychoanalysis from Freud to Lacan . . . I upheld that this was where the effective procedures of truth took place, on the basis of which philosophy strives to construct an original concept of what a truth is.

I maintain this system of conditions today. It has, however, become much less evident to illustrate. As regards the sciences, these are increasingly reduced to their impact on technologies' marketability. That covered by the word 'art' finds itself diluted between the weak idea of 'communication', the 'multimedia' aspiration to combine the whole array of sensorial means within new imaginary constructions, and the cultural relativism dissolving any and all norms. In fact, the word 'culture' seems bound to forbid little by little any clear usage of the word 'art'. Under the name of democracy, and following the collapse of State Communism, politics has been reduced, in general, to a sort of cross between economy and management, with a fair dose of police and control thrown in. As for love, this is, as I've mentioned, caught between a contractual conception of the family and a libertine conception of sexuality. To put things succinctly, let's say that technology, culture, management and sex have taken up the generic place of science, art, politics and love.

As a result, not only must we recall these conditions and their modern countenance, we also need to defend their active autonomy. This amounts, in fact, to setting them out in the contemporary historical development of their processes – a more descriptive than theoretical task, which I have not undertaken here. The avenues to explore are, however, fairly clear.

One would have to show that a new theoretical framework completely changes mathematical presentation – particularly, the mathematization of logic. This framework is the theory of categories. In the field of physics, the hypotheses that generalize relativity by considering every phenomenon to include, in its phenomenal particularity, the scale of its existence, are the most promising, and all the more so given that they have a solid, modern mathematical referent in fractal geometry.

As regards art, one would have to show how, following on the heels of cinema (the greatest artistic invention of the past century), new possibilities are springing up, without their exploration having, as yet, produced a decisive shift towards a fundamental reorganization of the classification and hierarchy of artistic activities. The advent of virtual images or images without any referent undoubtedly opens up a new stage of questions of representation. Here and now, in any case, the concentrated forms taken by painting – monumental included – indicate what is to be understood by the return of affirmation in art,[1] after decades of critical negation. Art can and must take a stand on History, take stock of the past century and propose new sensory forms of a thought that is not simply rebellious but also a force of unification around a number of affirmations that we might call 'sensible principles'.

In politics, the expansion (foreseen by Marx) of the global market modifies the transcendental (the world, the active arena) of emancipatory action, with it being perhaps only today that the conditions are assembled for a Communist International[2] that is neither state-controlled nor bureaucratic. In any case, two things are already clear from the ongoing political experiences that have drawn the consequences of the previous century's political history and have solid roots in the real of workers and the people: first, that it is possible to implement a politics that keeps its

122

distance from the State, with neither power as a stake nor parliamentarianism as its framework, and, second, that this politics proposes forms of organization that are far removed from the model of the party which dominated the entire twentieth century.[3]

Finally, one would have to inquire into the meaning of the fierce onslaught directed against psychoanalysis over the last ten or twenty years, at the same time as a type of bland normalization of sexual practices overall has taken place, and refer these facts to the transformation of amorous processes.

This labour is proposed to all . . .

3. In the first Manifesto, I named what I was trying to do a 'Platonic gesture', characterizing my philosophy by the paradoxical expression of a 'Platonism of the Multiple'. The reference to Plato remains fundamental in this second Manifesto but its orientation has changed. Twenty years ago, I wanted to call up Plato against the anti-Platonism of the entire twentieth century. In order to do so, I mobilized two themes: first, the reference to mathematics' ontological significance against the rhetorical and linguistic recourse to poetry characteristic of both modern

and ancient sophistry; and, second, the conviction that there exist truths which can be said to be 'absolute', with the ambitions of classical metaphysics being, in this sense, upheld against the leitmotif of its end or surpassing. Today, there are two additional themes reinforcing the Platonic affiliation which make their appearance. The first is the philosophical suspicion that must be cast on the pro-'democracy' propaganda that is as hegemonic today as it is belligerent. Plato proposed the first systematic critique of democracy and we have no alternative but to take that work up. Of course, the perspective from which we do so needs to be completely different but it is striking that Plato proposes, at least as regards the ruling aristocracy, a Communist type of solution. For the fundamental question facing the contemporary world could well be: either war-mongering capitalist-parliamentarianism (hence 'democracy') or the victorious renewal of the Communist hypothesis? The second new theme is that of the Idea. As we have seen in the preceding chapter, what I'm seeking to uphold is that the authentic life is a life marked by the Idea, and that Plato's dialectical construction can, in many respects, be interpreted along my lines. In the end, this second Manifesto is underpinned by the necessity of a second Platonic gesture; no longer the Platonism of the multiple (though this is still upheld) but *a Communism of the Idea*.

4. In *Being and Event*, as in the first Manifesto presenting the former's argument in a concentrated form, the fundamental concept was that of 'generic' – which is, moreover, the heading of the Manifesto's last chapter. This word indicated the main ontological characteristic of truths – namely, given that, like everything that is, their being qua being is pure multiplicity, truths are generic multiplicities. Amongst the multiplicities that make up a world (at the time I spoke of a 'situation'), they are characterized by their absence of characteristics. They testify for the whole world – which is why they are its truth – given that, unable to be defined by any particular predicate, their being can be considered to be identical to the simple fact of belonging to this world. It's in this sense that Marx upheld that the proletariat, stripped of everything except its labour power, represented generic humanity, with it thereby becoming the truth of the modern historico-political situation. I showed that the universality of truths, which are nonetheless created in particular worlds, is

Conclusion

connected precisely to their absence of particularities. The pivotal point was to demonstrate that generic multiplicities can exist – which is what a famous theorem by the mathematician Paul Cohen was called upon to do – and then to set as the norm for any activity that aims at producing truths (or universality, for it's the same thing) the capacity of creating, in disparate situations, generic subsets of these situations.

In this second Manifesto, the pivotal concept is that of the subjectivizable body. It is still a question of truths but what's important is no longer their being, thought in the mathematical formalism of generic multiplicities, but, rather, the material process of their appearing, existence and development in a given world, as well as the subjective type attached to this process. While the essence of a generic multiplicity is a *negative* universality (the absence of any predicative identity) the essence of a body of truth resides in certain capacities – in particular, the capacity to deal with a whole series of *points* in the real. What is a point? It's a crucial moment of a body's development, when choosing one orientation rather than another decides its fate. If one likes, it's the contraction of the whole process into a simple alternative: this *or* that. In order to deal victoriously with such a point, the body has to have at its disposal what I name appropriate 'organs'. For example, to stand up to the onslaught of the armed counter-revolution, a revolutionary party (in the Leninist political sequence) requires a military type of organizational discipline. This discipline is the appropriate organ of the political body when the decision must be made (as is shown in Lenin's text 'The Crisis Is Ripe') to choose, affirmatively, either to insurrect or to wait-and-see. Alternatively, when Jackson Pollock decided, against the entire expressive or imitative tradition, to make painting directly transitive to the gesture of painting rather than to any sort whatsoever of objective or sentimental referent, he had to avail himself of not only surfaces and instruments by which to project suitable colours but also a sort of corporeal disposition orientated towards energetic rapidity and a saturation of the instant. Such are the organs of the pictorial truth of the *action painting* type.

In the end, then, one sees that the complex formed by the body, subjective orientation, points and organs, assembles in this second Manifesto an *affirmative* vision of universality. While the generic designates what a truth *is* in so far as it is distinguished from all other types of being, the body and its orientation designate what a truth *does* and, hence, the way in which it shares – even while parting from – the fate of objects in the world. The first Manifesto rests, as regards truths, upon a separatist doctrine of being; the second, upon an integrative doctrine of doing. To an ontology of true-universality there succeeds a pragmatic of its becoming.

5. At the moment of the first Manifesto and in the following years up to, no doubt, the mid-nineties, the battle raged around the universality of truths. My three books that were the most read from this sequence consist, in addition to the above-mentioned Manifesto, of my essay on Saint Paul (*Saint Paul or the Foundation of Universalism*) and the small manual entitled *Ethics*. The core point around which all these texts turned was the opposition between the cult of particularity, including the 'democratic' apologia for the individual, and the universal and generic dimension of truths. It is in this sense, moreover, that I spoke of an 'ethics of truths', which I radically opposed to both cultural relativism and the logomachy of human rights.

For some years now, as is particularly clear from various passages of *Logics of Worlds*, I have more readily emphasized truths' *eternity*. This is because universality is a question of form (the form of generic multiplicity) whereas eternity has to do with the process's effective result. What interests me is that a truth is produced with particular materials in a specific world, yet, at the same time, since it is understood and usable in an entirely different world and across potentially vast spans of time – we understand the artistic power of cave paintings executed 40,000 years ago – it has, well and truly, to be trans-temporal. I call truths' 'eternity' this inviolate availability making it possible for them to be resuscitated and reactivated in worlds heterogeneous to those in which they were created, and crossing over, as such, unknown oceans and obscure millennia. It's absolutely necessary that theory be able to account for this migration. It has to explain how ideal existences, often materialized in objects, can both be created at a precise point of space-time and possess this form of eternity. Descartes spoke of the 'creation of eternal truths'. I'm taking up this programme but without the help of God . . .

When all is said and done, this second Manifesto

is the result of our confused and detestable present time forcing us to declare that there are eternal truths in politics, art, science and love. And that if we are armed with this conviction, if we understand that to participate, point by point, in the process of creation of subjectivizable bodies is what renders life more powerful than survival, we will possess what Rimbaud, at the end of *A Season in Hell*, desired above all else: 'Truth, in a soul and a body'. Then shall we be stronger than Time.

Notes

Translator's Preface: A Manifest Power of Elevation!

1 Deleuze, Gilles, *Critique et Clinique* (Paris: Minuit, 1993), p. 141.

2 Derrida, Jacques, 'The Double Session', in *Dissemination*, trans. Barbara Johnson (Chicago: University of Chicago Press, 1981), p. 220. Translation modified.

3 Badiou, A., 'Français: De la langue française comme évidement', in Barbara Cassin (ed.), *Vocabulaire européen des philosophies* (Paris: Editions du Seuil/ Dictionnaires Le Robert, 2004), p. 471.

4 Ibid., p. 468.

5 See: Badiou, Alain, 'Author's Preface', to his *Being and Event*, trans. Oliver Feltham (London: Continuum, 2005), p. xiv.

6 See: Nancy, Jean-Luc, *The Speculative Remark: One of Hegel's Bons Mots,* trans. Céline Surprenant (Stanford: Stanford University Press, 2001), and

Büttgen, Philippe, 'Aufheben, Aufhebung', in Barbara Cassin (ed.), *Vocabulaire européen des philosophies* (op.cit.).

7 Hegel, Georg Wilhelm Friedrich, *Science of Logic*, trans. A. V. Miller, ed. M. George and A. Vincent (Oxford: Blackwell, 1986), paragraphs 184–7.

8 See, most notably: Derrida, Jacques, 'What is a "Relevant" Translation?', trans. Lawrence Venturi, *Critical Inquiry* 27 (2001): 174–200. Originally published as: 'Qu'est-ce qu'une traduction "relevante"?', *Quinzièmes Assises de la Traduction Littéraire (Arles, 1998)* (Arles: Actes Sud, 1999), and re-published in *Derrida* (Paris: L'Herne, 2004), pp. 561–76. Derrida also refers to the untranslatability of *aufheben* in Christie V. McDonald (ed.), *The Ear of the Other: Otobiography, Transference and Translation. Texts and Discussions with Jacques Derrida*, trans. Peggy Kamuf (New York: Schocken Books, 1985), pp. 127–8.

9 Suchting, Wallis Arthur, 'Some Minority Comments on Terminology', in G. W .F. Hegel, *The Encyclopaedia Logic. Part I of the Encyclopaedia of Philosophical Sciences with the Zusätze*, translated by T. F. Geraets, W. A. Suchting and H. S. Harris (Indianapolis, Indiana: Hackett Publishing Company, 1991), p. xxxv.

10 Badiou, Alain, 'Français: De la langue française comme évidement' (op. cit.).

11 Labarrière, Pierre-Jean, 'Sursumer/sursomption', in Gwendoline Jarczyk and Pierre-Jean Labarrière, *Hegeliana* (Paris: Presses Universitaires de France, 1986), pp. 102–20. Cited in Büttgen, Philippe (loc. cit.).

12 Badiou, Alain, *Being and Event* (op.cit.), p. 488.

13 We might note in this respect Badiou's stipulation, in his article on the French language, that philosophy is 'a matter of speaking the language common "to everyone" and therefore, given we are in France, French, without charging this with special considerations concerning either concepts (which are, in themselves, indifferent to language) or language (for French has no particular privilege because of this)' (loc. cit.), p. 466.

14 Badiou, Alain, *Being and Event* (op.cit.), p. 488.

15 I'm relying here on: Rey, Alain (ed.), *Dictionnaire culturel en langue française* (Paris: Dictionnaires le Robert, 2005); the Robert-Collins English/French dictionary (Glasgow and Paris: HarperCollins and Dictionnaires le Robert, 6th edn, 2002); and *Le Trésor de la langue française informatisé* (<http://atilf.atilf.fr>).

16 Derrida, Jacques, 'The Pit and the Pyramid', *Margins of Philosophy*, trans. Alan Bass (Chicago: Chicago University Press, 1982).

17 Derrida, Jacques, 'What is a "Relevant" Translation?' (loc.cit.), p. 196.

18 The clearest example here is the following passage: 'In 1967, to translate a crucial German word with a double meaning (*Aufheben*, *Aufhebung*), a word that signifies at once to suppress and to elevate [...], a word which everyone had until then agreed was untranslatable – or, if you prefer, a word concerning which no two people in the world could agree as to how to translate it in a stable, satisfactory way into any language – I proposed the noun "relève" or the verb "relever". This allowed me to retain, joining them in a single word, the double motif of the elevation and the replacement that preserves that which it denies or suppresses, preserving that which it causes to disappear, quite like – in a perfect example – what is called in the armed forces, in the navy, say, "the changing of the guard" *[la relève de la garde]*' (ibid. (translation modified)).

19 See Derrida, Jacques, 'Positions. Interview with Jean-Louis Houdebine and Guy Scarpetta', in *Positions*, trans. Alan Bass (London: Athlone Press, 1981), pp. 40–1. (Originally published in *Positions* (Paris: Minuit, 1972).)

20 This seems an obvious point to make but one should note that *aufheben* has also been translated

into French by a bevy of terms having absolutely no resonance of 'raising up', such as: *abroger, abolir,* and *dépasser* (the literal translations of which are, respectively, 'abrogate', 'abolish', and 'exceed'). The sense of 'to raise up' is also less evident in neologisms such as *sursumer* or *sur-primer.*

21 While Derrida's translators have predominantly chosen to leave the terms *relever/relève,* when used in their technical sense, untranslated, various English renderings have been proposed, though not always explicitly given that many figure 'surreptitiously' within the very texts whose translators have opted for the principle of non-translation. In the case of the verb, one finds: 'relay', 'relieve' and 'put into relief', in addition to 'relift', 'lift up' and 'raise up'. We might add that, in the case of Derrida's article on translation to which we have referred several times in this preface, the translator, Lawrence Venturi, at times renders the French term expansively, effectively glossing it by a cluster of verbs: for example, 'elevates, preserves and negates', or again 'elevates and interiorizes, thereby preserving and negating' (see here: Venturi, L., 'Translating Derrida on Translation: Relevance and Disciplinary Resistance', *The Yale Journal of Criticism* 16/2 (2003): 255–6).

22 See infra.: p. 61.

23 See Badiou, Alain, 'Beyond Formalisation', interview with Bruno Bosteels and Peter Hallward (2004): <http://ciepfc.rhapsodyk.net/article.php3?id_article=48>, p. 18.

24 See here: infra. p. 84; 'Beyond Formalisation' (loc. cit.), p. 18; and Badiou, Alain, and Truong, Nicholas, *Eloge de l'amour* (Paris: Flammarion, 2009), p. 63.

25 See: Badiou, A., *Logics of Worlds*, trans. Alberto Toscano (London: Continuum, 2009), p. 391.

26 Ibid., p. 378; my emphasis.

27 Badiou, Alain, with Tarby, Fabien, *La Philosophie et l'événement. Entretiens* (Paris: Editions Germina, 2010), pp. 146–7.

28 Ibid., p. 147.

29 Infra., p. 62.

30 See here the chapter on Hegel in *Logics of Worlds* (op. cit.), pp. 141–52.

31 Cf. note 21 supra.

32 Infra., p. 84.

33 *Logics of Worlds* (op. cit.), p. 379.

0: Introduction

1 *Trans. note:* That the entire history of philosophy must be thought in terms of 'moments', considered not as discrete stages dialectically framed within a teleological movement leading up to the present but as determined, historical sequences

articulated around no less determined philosophical problems, is argued by Frédéric Worms in his
book on twentieth-century French philosophy,
La Philosophie en France au XXe siècle. Moments
(Paris: Gallimard, 2009). While Worms's book
was published the same year as Badiou's *Second
Manifesto*, its analyses of three distinct moments in
twentieth-century French philosophy had been outlined in a variety of publications and conferences
presented by Worms from the mid-1990s on. In
his capacity as director of the International Centre
for the Study of Contemporary French Philosophy
(CIEPFC), at the Ecole Normale Supérieure – a
position previously held by Badiou – Worms has,
moreover, overseen the organization of numerous colloquia dealing with French philosophical
'moments', amongst which was a series in 2008 con-
secrated specifically to the 'moment of the sixties'
and exploring, respectively, its epistemological,
metaphysical, political and aesthetic dimensions.
Badiou, for his part, presents what he views as the
'programme' defining the philosophical 'moment'
elaborated in France between the publication of
Sartre's *Being and Nothingness* (1943) and Deleuze
and Guattari's *What is Philosophy?* (1991), in 'The
Adventure of French Philosophy', *New Left Review*
35 (September–October 2005).

2   *Trans. note:* In English in the original.
3   There exists in France a vigorous generation of true philosophers – neither parrots of the portable morality, nor sentinels of soporific sciences – all of whom are roughly in their mid-thirties. As for the older generation, there are many who ensure that the munificent years still radiate on the public scene even if they differ amongst themselves as to the nature and references of this munificence. The situation is even better in other countries, where the initial French impetus was sustained for much longer. It is not, then, the moment to despair. The game is being played out on the level, firstly, of what is transmitted, which presupposes something other than communication or academism, and, secondly, of the ways in which this transmission is transformed, which presupposes a new contemporaneity. The two processes are sufficiently under way for us to know that the dominant alliance of scientism and phenomenology – that is, of restrictive 'reality' and vulgar morality – will be vanquished.
4   *Manifeste pour la philosophie* (Paris: Le Seuil, 1989). This book has been translated:

    – into English, by Norman Madarasz (New York: State University of New York Press, 1999);

– into Spanish, by V. Alcantud (Madrid: Catedra, 1989);

– into Danish, by K. Hyldgaard and O. Petersen (Arhus: Slagmark, 1991);

– into Portuguese, by M. D. Magno (Rio de Janeiro: Angélica, 1991);

– into Italian, by F. Elefante (Milan: Feltrinelli, 1991);

– into German, by J. Wolf and E. Hoerl (Vienna: Turia & Kant, 1998);

– into Korean (Seoul, 2000);

– into Croatian, by Naklada Jesenski i Turk (Zagreb, 2001);

– into Russian, by V. E. Lapitsky (St Petersburg: Machina, 2003);

– into Slovenian, by R. Riha and J. Sumic-Riha (Ljubljana: Zalozba ZRC, 2004);

– into Japanese (Tokyo, 2004);

– into Swedish, by D. Moaven Doust (Stockholm: Glänta production, 2005);

– into Turkish, by Nilgün Tutal and Hakki Hünler (2005);

– into Greek, by Ada Klabatséa and Vlassis Skolidis (Athens: Psichogios Pub, 2006).

I would like to note in passing that almost all the living philosophers, my contemporaries, referred to in this first Manifesto have since died: Deleuze,

Derrida, Lacoue-Labarthe, Lyotard . . . Some idea of what tied me to them can be gleaned from the *Pocket Pantheon* (entitled in French: *Petit Panthéon portatif*) that I published in 2008 with La Fabrique, whose director is my friend Eric Hazan. (The English translation, by David Macey, was published by Verso [London and New York] in 2009.)

5 On this point, one may consult the dossier that I coordinated with Cécile Winter, 'Portées du mot "juif"' ('The Uses of the Word "Jew"'), as the third of the *Circonstances* series that I have published over the last five years with the publishers Lignes, managed by my friend Michel Surya. (See: 'The Uses of the Word "Jew"', in *Polemics*, trans. Steve Corcoran, London and New York: Verso, 2006.)

6 *Trans. note: Logics of Worlds*, the English translation of Badiou's second volume of *Being and Event*, was published in 2009 (trans. Alberto Toscano, London: Continuum), while the English translation of the first volume, by Oliver Feltham, was published in 2005 (also by Continuum).

0.1: Outline

1 I like the great metaphors hailing from religion: Miracle, Grace, Salvation, Glorious Body, Conversion . . . This has, predictably enough, led

to the conclusion that my philosophy is a disguised Christianity. The book I published on St Paul in 1997 did not help matters (*Saint Paul or the Foundation of Universalism*, trans. R. Brassier, Stanford: Stanford University Press, 2003; originally published as *Saint Paul ou la fondation de l'universalisme*, Paris: Presses universitaires de la France, 1997). That said, all in all I would rather be a revolutionary atheist cloaked in a religious vocabulary than a Western 'democrat'-cum-persecutor of Muslim men and women, disguised as a secular feminist.

2   This point is most fully developed in the conclusion of *Logics of Worlds* (op. cit.), 'What is Living?' Although it concentrates a large and complex book, this text is essentially comprehensible on its own.

Chapter 1: Opinion

1   *Trans. note:* That the pronouns 'him' and 'he' are employed here and in what follows for 'the philosopher' is neither in contravention to non-sexist language usage nor tacitly in compliance with Alain Badiou's stipulation elsewhere – in his presentation to the dialogue between Nicolas Truong and himself, *Eloge de l'amour* (Paris: Flammarion, 2009) – that when he uses the 'neutral term' 'he' for

'the philosopher' one must also, naturally, understand 'she'. The pronouns are simply contextually
motivated given that the position defended by the
philosopher is Badiou's own.

One might, however, note that, while Badiou's
text as a whole conforms to the standard French
practice of using only masculine ('neutral') pronouns and articles (*'le' philosophe* and not *'le ou la'*
philosophe, for example), there are two occasions
on which he specifically includes 'the feminine':
the first is found in n.1 of 0.1: Outline, above,
where it is a question of Western democrats' perse-
cution of 'Muslim men and women' (*musulman(e)*
s in French), and the second in the chapter
on Subjectivation, where one occurrence of the
French word for 'lover' amalgamates both the masculine and the feminine variants: *amant(e)*. In this
latter case, the English translation is simply 'lover'.

2   The four types of 'generic procedures', to employ
the jargon developed in *Being and Event* (op. cit.)
– namely, politics, love, the arts and the sciences
– are unable to be rationally deduced as the only
possible types of human production capable of
laying claim to a certain universality. But the other
propositions which have not failed to eventuate
(work, religion, law and so on) are in no way satisfactory, in my view. Several detailed studies of the

four fundamental types can be found in *Conditions* (trans. Steve Corcoran, New York: Continuum, 2008; originally published as *Conditions,* Paris: Le Seuil, 1992) and, above all, in the three books originally published in 1998: *Briefings on Existence: A Short Treatise on Transitory Ontology* (trans. Norman Madarasz, Albany: State University of New York Press, 2006; originally published as *Court traité d'ontologie transitoire*, Paris: Le Seuil, 1998), *Metapolitics* (trans. Jason Barker, London and New York: Verso, 2005; originally published as *Abrégé de métapolitique*, Paris: Le Seuil, 1998), and *Handbook of Inaesthetics* (trans. Alberto Toscano, Stanford: Stanford University Press, 2005; originally published as *Petit manuel d'inesthétique*, Paris: Le Seuil, 1998).

3   See the last chapter of *Briefings on Existence: A Short Treatise on Transitory Ontology* (op. cit.) for the most accessible introduction to this equivalence between the theory of appearing and logic.

Chapter 2: Appearance

1   *Trans. note:* André Malraux's *Le Musée imaginaire* (Paris: Gallimard, 1965) has been translated into English under the title of *Museum Without Walls* (trans. Stuart Gilbert and Francis Price, New York: Doubleday & Company, 1967).

2   *Trans. note:* The verses, in French, are 'Tu penches, grand platane, et te proposes nu / Blanc comme un jeune Scythe. / Mais ta candeur est prise et ton pied retenu / Par la force du site.'

This is the first stanza of Paul Valéry's 'Au Platane' ('To the Plane Tree'), in *Charmes* (Paris: Gallimard, 1922).

Chapter 3: Differentiation

1   *Trans. note:* The French collocation that has been translated here as 'the daydreamer in the valley' is 'le dormeur du val', which, as its more literal translation 'the sleeper in the valley' indicates, is the title of a poem by Rimbaud.

2   This structure is, as a result, as fundamental in philosophy as is that of sets. Indeed, it plays the same role for the logic of appearing as does the axiomatic of sets for the ontology of multiplicities. Let me therefore present it here, by way of this book's sole foray into formalisms:

   a.   One has a set T, named a set of degrees or transcendental of the world. The elements of this set will be named uniformly 'degrees'. 'Degree' abbreviates 'degree of identity between two multiples that appear in the world of which T is the transcendental'. The degrees are denoted: $p, q, r, s, t \ldots$

144

b. An order relation, classically written as ≤, is defined on the set T. Such a relation, it should be recalled, is:

- Transitive: if $p \leq q$ and $q \leq r$, then $p \leq r$,
- Reflexive: $p \leq p$,
- Anti-symmetrical: if $p \leq q$ and $q \leq p$, then $p = q$.

If two degrees of T, p and q, are linked by the relation ≤ (which is in no way obligatory), as with $p \leq q$, for example, one says that 'p is less than or equal to q' or, equally, that 'q is greater than or equal to p'. If two degrees are not linked by ≤, they are said to be incomparable.

c. There exists in T a minimal degree, denoted μ, which is less than or equal to any degree of T. In other words, for any p of T, one has $\mu \leq p$. There also exists a maximum degree, denoted M, which is greater than or equal to any degree of T. In other words, for any p of T, one has $p \leq M$.

d. There exists a binary operation, conjunction, denoted ∩, which, when applied to two degrees p and q of T, yields the element $r = p \cap q$, such that this is the largest of the elements that are simultaneously less than both *p* and *q*. In other words, first one has $p \cap q \leq$ *p* and $p \cap q \leq q$ and, secondly, if one has $t \leq p$ and $t \leq q$, then $t \leq p \cap q$.

e. For any set A of transcendental degrees – that is, $A \subseteq T - $, even infinite, there exists an element Env(A), called the envelope of A, that is the smallest of all the elements of T that are greater than or equal to all the elements of A. In other words, on the one hand, Env(A) is a degree greater than or equal to all the degrees that are elements of A and, on the other hand, if p is a degree of T greater than or equal to all the degrees that are elements of A, one has Env(A) $\leq p$.

f. The (finite) operation *conjunction* $\cap$ is distributive in relation to the (infinite) operation *envelope* Env. In other words, the conjunction of an element *p* with the envelope of a subset of T, let's say A, is equal to the envelope of the conjunction of *p* with all the degrees that are elements of A. This can be written as:

$$[p \cap \text{Env(A)}] = \text{Env} [(p \cap t)/t \in A].$$

It is remarkable that such a simple structure be capable of serving as the basis for the

146

formalization of a complete theory of appearing and of worlds.

3   *Trans. note:* In English in the original.

4   The dialectical opposition between algebra and topology is at the core of my *Theory of the Subject* (trans. Bruno Bosteels, New York: Continuum, 2009; originally published as *Théorie du sujet*, Paris: Le Seuil, 1982).

5   As regards Wittgenstein, one can read the small book *L'Antiphilosophie de Wittgenstein*, published in 2009 by the Éditions Nous, managed by my friend Benoît Casas.

Chapter 4: Existence

1   On the important notion of 'thing', it is certainly necessary to read Heidegger's 'What is a Thing?' (trans. W. B. Barton, Jr. and Vera Deutsch, Chicago: Henry Regnery Company, 1967), as well as the very fine text by Jean-Luc Nancy, 'The Heart of Things' (in *The Birth to Presence*, trans. Brian Holmes and others, Stanford: Stanford University Press, 1993).

4.1 Philosophy's Existence

1   *Trans. note:* As discussed in the translator's preface, the verb 'to raise up' and the nominal variant

'raising up' render, respectively, the French *relever* and *relève* – terms proposed by Jacques Derrida as translations of Hegel's *aufheben* and *Aufhebung*, usually rendered in English as 'to sublate' and 'sublation'. I would recall here that the choice of an 'everyday expression' – 'to raise up' – rather than a 'technical term' – 'to sublate' – as a translation for *relever / aufheben* is in conformity with Badiou's own decision to employ Derrida's rendering of the German rather than the term proposed by the translators of Hegel into French. Hence Badiou's note in *Being and Event*: 'I was not able to reconcile myself to translating *aufheben* by *sursumer* [the term proposed by P.-J. Labarrière and G. Jarczyk in their translation of Hegel's *Logic*] . . . because the substitution of a technical neologism in one language for an everyday word from another language appears to me to be a renunciation rather than a victory. I have thus taken up J. Derrida's suggestion: *relever, relève*' (*Being and Event*, op. cit., p. 488). The various senses encapsulated by the verb 'to raise up' which render it an appropriate translation of *relever / aufheben* are specified in the translator's preface.

2   *Trans. note:* The word 'reckless' here – as is also the case for the occurrences that follow – is in English in the original.

Chapter 5: Mutation

1   *Trans. note:* In French: *un site (se) fait apparaître lui-même*. Badiou's sentence enfolds a variety of permutations, each of which comprises a cluster of different senses. When read, for example, without the bracketed reflexive pronoun 'se', the clause – 'un site fait apparaître lui-même' – may be translated as either, or both:

- a site makes itself appear;
- a site is (constitutes) appearing itself.

Both these renderings in English would, however, be more commonly expressed in French by the reflexive construction 'se fait apparaître' – such as is, in fact, yielded by Badiou's clause were one to make abstraction of the pronominal, reflexive form 'lui-même' ('itself') positioned after the verb. In other words the clause 'un site se fait apparaître' equally means either, or both:

- a site makes itself appear;
- a site is (constitutes, or becomes) appearing itself.

To which, moreover, a third sense needs to be added, namely:

- a site is made to appear.

As such, the permutations encompassed by
Badiou's sentence ('un site (se) fait apparaître
lui-même') pivot upon, and self-referentially play
themselves out between, the 'double reflexivity'
therein inscribed – which is a way of highlight-
ing, of course, the critical characteristic by which a
site forms an exception to the laws both of being
and of appearing: namely, that of its reflexivity.
As Badiou puts it a little later on, this reflexivity
entails that the 'site belongs to itself, at least fleetingly, such that its multiple-being comes to the
surface of its appearing "in person"'. Ordinarily,
that is, multiple-being, qua the ontological support
for objects appearing in the world, does not itself
appear; in the case of a site, however, this basis
in being rises to the surface of objectivity as a
consequence of itself falling under the measurement of its elements' identity by which appearing
is brought about. The double role that thereby
accrues to the multiple in question is expressed
by Badiou in *Logics of Worlds* as follows: 'First, it is
objectivated by the transcendental indexing of its
elements. Second, it (self-)objectivates by figuring
among its elements and by thus being caught up in
the transcendental indexing of which it is the ontological support' (op.cit., p. 360). That it is also possible to hear in the term 'apparaître' ('to appear' or

'appearing') the semi-homophonic 'être' ('to be' or 'being') may, in this respect, be seen to underscore the fact that, with the site's basis in being acceding to appearing as well, being and appearing are, fleetingly, inseparably 'superimposed' or 'fused'.

The English rendering of Badiou's sentence, 'a site itself is made to appear (of itself)', seeks, as such, to enfold the different senses discussed above in its various rhythmic accentuations or grammatical permutations:

- A site itself is *made to appear* – as with any multiple, a site only exists or appears in so far as a transcendental assignation of a degree takes place. The passive construction here aims at capturing, therefore, the sense of the multiple's 'objectivation' by the transcendental indexing of its elements, such as this constitutes 'appearing' itself.
- A site *itself* is made to appear – the multiple's basis in *being* comes locally to the surface as an exception to the fundamental ontological law prohibiting any multiple from being an element of itself.
- A site itself is made to appear *of itself* – it is by falling itself under the measurement of identities applied to its elements that a

multiple itself appears or 'self-objectivates' – such that it assigns to its own being a value of existence.

2   *Trans. note:* The verses, in French, are '–Non ! dit l'arbre. Il dit *Non* ! par l'étincellement / de sa tête superbe, / Que la tempête traite universellement / Comme elle fait une herbe.'

This is the last stanza of Paul Valéry's 'Au Platane', in *Charmes* (op. cit).

Chapter 6: Incorporation

1   *Trans. note:* The French clause translated as 'the in-corporated (and reiterated: 'encore!') unfurling of its effects' is *'le déploiement en corps ("encore!") de ses effets'*. The collocation 'en corps' – which has the sense both of 'in body' and 'in a corps', in the latter's acceptation of 'an aggregate of persons' – is a homonym with the 'encore' between brackets, which, in addition to its sense of 'again', echoes the title of Lacan's *Seminar XX: Encore.*

2   On love, one may read two texts: 'What is love?' (in *Conditions*, op. cit.) and 'The Scene of the Two' (trans. Barbara P. Fulks, *lacanian ink* 21, 2003). (Trans-note: To these texts, one might add the dialogue between Badiou and Nicolas Truong, *Eloge de l'amour* ['In Praise of Love'], op. cit.)

Chapter 7: Subjectivation

1   *Trans. note:* In English in the original.
2   The temptation makes its appearance today of an unprincipled alliance between a so-called 'extreme left' viewpoint, on the one hand, and the loose conglomeration of small, fascistic groups of an Islamic veneer, on the other. The West's 'extreme left' is fascinated, in its powerlessness, by these small groups' power to create havoc and the attendant media fuss. Such an alliance, however, apart from the fact that it is unacceptable, has absolutely no future. It would demoralize those engaged in building a new type of popular politics as surely as the Germano-Soviet pact demoralized Communist militants between 1939 and 1941.

   Note within the note: I am not confusing here what I call 'small, fascistic groups of an Islamic veneer' with organizations that, while equally religious ones – and none of whose principles I share – can, nevertheless, be observed to have firm national roots and a constituted mass audience, such as the Hamas in Palestine or the Hezbollah in Lebanon. The Taliban in Afghanistan and the Islamic Courts in Somalia are no doubt intermediary cases whose political future is undetermined.

3   *Trans. note:* See: Merleau-Ponty, *Adventures of*

the Dialectic (1955, trans. Joseph Bien, London: Heinemann, 1974).

Chapter 8: Ideation

1 *Trans. note:* The passage of *The Republic* presented here is 509b. As is evident from the context, the translation given in the text is of Badiou's own translation from the Greek.

2 I am still today particularly susceptible to what I have called 'the enchantment of the place of the Number'. I dedicated to this what is perhaps, among my theoretical works, the one I prefer: *Number and Numbers* (trans. Robin Mackay, Cambridge: Polity; originally published as *Le Nombre et les nombres*, Paris: Le Seuil, 1990). In this book, I particularly give a detailed presentation of all that intimately binds the theme of the actual infinite to the generic concept of 'number', turning upside down in this way both the old problematic of finitude and Hegel's 'bad infinite'.

Conclusion

1 Regarding the return of affirmation in art and the aesthetic doctrine related to it, one can read 'Third Sketch of a Manifesto of Affirmationist Art' (trans. Steve Corcoran, in *Polemics*, op. cit.;

originally published as: 'Troisième esquisse d'un manifeste de l'affirmationisme', *Circonstances* 2, Paris: Lignes, 2004).

2   The words 'Communism' and 'Communists' must be taken in the generic sense they have in the work of the young Marx. For historical reasons, this sense was, to a great extent, overlaid in the twentieth century by the resonance imparted to the word in expressions such as 'Communist Party' or 'International Communist movement'. As we are in the era of politics without party – which shows, incidentally, that the creation of an 'anti-capitalist party' is an abortive enterprise, in the sense that it is immediately absorbed by capitalist-parliamentarianism – 'Communism' must no longer be thought as the adjective attached to 'party' but, quite to the contrary, as a regulatory hypothesis enveloping the variable fields and new organiza-tions of emancipatory politics. Regarding all this, see my small book *The Meaning of Sarkozy* (trans. David Fernbach, New York: Verso, 2008; originally published as *De quoi Sarkozy est-il le nom?*, Paris: Nouvelles Editions Lignes, 2008), especially chap-ters 8 and 9.

3   As concerns the political experimentation that is the most significant along these lines in France, see the publications of the *Organisation politique*

and the *Rassemblement des Collectifs des Ouvriers Sans Papiers des Foyers*. I recommend in this respect the collected issues of *Le Journal politique*. Write to the following address: Le Perroquet, BP 84, 75462, Paris, Cedex 10, France, and also: journal.politique@laposte.net.

Index

Index

Index

Index

Index